John Matthias was born in 1941 in Columbus, Ohio. For many years he taught at the University of Notre Dame, but also spent long periods of time in the UK, both at Cambridge and at his wife's childhood home in Hacheston, Suffolk. He has been a Visiting Fellow in poetry at Clare Hall, Cambridge, and is now a Life Member. Until 2012 he was poetry editor of *Notre Dame Review* and is now Editor at Large. Matthias has published some thirty books of poetry, translation, scholarship, and collaboration. Shearsman has published his three volumes of *Collected Poems*, 2011, 2012, and 2013, along with two books of essays, *Who Was Cousin Alice? And Other Questions* and *At Large*, the long poem *Trigons*, and his last collection of shorter poems, *Complayntes for Doctor Neuro*. Two volumes of collaborative work have recently appeared from Dos Madres, *Revolutions*, with printmaker Jean Dibble and critic Robert Archambeau, and *Regrounding a Pilgrimage*, with poet and Jungian scholar John Peck. Simultaneous with the publication of *Acoustic Shadows*, Ars Interpres in Sweden is publishing a selection of shorter and longer poems translated by Lars-Håkan Svensson, *Nordlig Sommar*. Matthias's work has also been translated into a number of other languages. Collections of critical essays on Matthias's poetry include *Word Play Place*, edited by Robert Archambeau, and *The Salt Companion to John Matthias*, edited by Joe Francis Doerr.

Also by John Matthias

Poetry
Bucyrus (1970)
Turns (1975)
Crossing (1979)
Bathory & Lermontov (1980)
Northern Summer (1984)
A Gathering of Ways (1991)
Swimming at Midnight (1995)
Beltane at Aphelion (1995)
Pages: New Poems & Cuttings (2000)
Working Progress, Working Title (2002)
Swell & Variations on the Song of Songs (2003)
New Selected Poems (2004)
Kedging (2007)
Trigons (2010) *
Collected Shorter Poems, Vol. 2 (2011) *
Collected Longer Poems (2012) *
Collected Shorter Poems, Vol. 1 (2013) *
Complayntes for Doctor Neuro & other poems (2016) *

Translations
Contemporary Swedish Poetry (1980) (with Göran Printz-Påhlson)
Jan Östergren: Rainmaker (1983) (with Göran Printz-Påhlson)
The Battle of Kosovo (1987) (with Vladeta Vučković)
Three-Toed Gull: Selected Poems of Jesper Svenbro (2003)
(with Lars-Håkan Svensson)

Prose
Reading Old Friends (1992)
Who Was Cousin Alice? and Other Questions (2011) *
Different Kinds of Music (2014) *
At Large (2016) *

Editions
23 Modern British Poets (1971)
Introducing David Jones (1980)
David Jones: Man and Poet (1989)
Selected Works of David Jones (1992)
Notre Dame Review: The First Ten Years (2009) (with William O'Rourke)

(* *indicates a Shearsman publication*)

John Matthias

Acoustic Shadows

Shearsman Books

First published in the United Kingdom in 2019 by
Shearsman Books
50 Westons Hill Drive
Emersons Green
BRISTOL
BS16 7DF

Shearsman Books Ltd Registered Office
3 - 1 St. James Place, Mangotsfield, Bristol BS16 9JB
(this address not for correspondence)

www.shearsman.com

ISBN 978-1-84861-636-3

Acknowledgements
Some of these poems have been published in the following print and on
line publications: *Salmagundi, Parnassus, The Common,
Notre Dame Review* and *X-Peri*.

The author is grateful to Jean Dibble, printmaker and painter,
for the cover art. Dibble has exhibited extensively, both internationally
and in the US since 1978. Recent years have been spent integrating
text and image, as well as delving into portraiture. One of the founding
members of the Mid America Print council, a group dedicated to
fostering the best in printmaking via conferences, exhibitions, and
research, she has been active in the organization for most of
its existence. She collaborated with John Matthias and Robert
Archambeau on the Dos Madres book *Revolutions* (2017).

Contents

For Michael Anania and Peter Michelson

Fifty years of conversation

PROLOGUE

After Carlos Drummond de Andrade's "Lembrança do Mundo Antigo"

I used to walk with friends in the ravine.
The sky was caught in the trees, and the trees
Were blue, the sky was green. The water
Under the bridge had dried to large puddles
Where we floated little boats. There were no rules
That told us to stay dry. We went home wet.
We went home late to dinners that our mothers
Had to warm for us. Nobody got mad.

Nobody got mad or shouted in those days.
Our cap guns only made a little bang. Real guns,
They told us, would now be turned to plows
And children's toys. A great war had ended.
Summer heat brought quiet fears whispered
By adults who loved us: polio, insect bites,
Or that we might get lost. We easily survived.

Old cars and broken bikes were sometimes left
Behind a stand of trees. We'd pretend to fix the cars,
And really fix the bikes. We stood up tall or crouched.
Carlos Drummond de Andrade,
We went down there early in the morning.
Like you, we had mornings in those days.

I

'Stanza'
and
Other Stanzas

Stanza

untitled, un-
finished drawing from around
1540 is anonymous
and delicate and tentative and so
worn as almost not
to be there   and if I should
breathe on it I'm sure
the thing that hovers near non-being
would disintegrate   detach
itself from paper to inhabit air as motes
of graphite possibly to cause
infection of the lungs upon my in-
halation   therefore some unknown
authorities have caused
a thin glass to
intervene between the thing's ancient
image – profile of a woman? – and
our invading curiosity

Elevenses

My dna is better than
your dna. Also bigger.
Dana, you think you're
a slugger. Bugger that.
Dinah is from North
Carolina. Nothing's finer
than my kgb that's
Better than your kgb.
And richer, slicker.
Anagrammed, the dna is
Only *and*, but quicker.

*

My fbi is cooler than your
fbi. Crookeder deletes
the straighter every time.
Hotter in pursuit is never
fast as just to stand in wait.
Who also serve. A warrant.
A currant bun. Secret is
Your ibf is bluff. Never heard
of it? Well that's the point.
The joints are out of time.
My nickel or your dime.

Prayer

Oh God please give me some money
and other things I want & that's my
prayer   and good sex and oh good
god some trouble for my enemies
I hate them and I voted for Trump

On the other hand the devout man's
neighbor simply plonks his banjo
on the porch while, down at the local
hall, a string quartet plays Haydn,
inventor of a hush of holy sound . . .

Short Poem about Politics

In politics, I vote for sanity and reason.
And passion, too. Yes, of course passion.
But the passion ought to be for sanity
And reason.

As for poetry, things are different there.

It Was Said

I

Ekstasis – it was said – or was that
ekphrasis – ? A lean meme of X or Y
explains all nothings coming at
you going in to stand unstill: Why

not say you exit in those words
instead of only looks –? Still stand-
ing, step away and lean in toward
a henge of stone and with thin wand

go wreck or wound whatever magic
into majesty. It's in your only hand.
Beside yourself and feeling tragic,
You amaze us even without mind-

ing or amending – any bloody one.
Come, come! said Mr. It Was Said.
I'll word your silent image, loan
You stasis, phrasic in your narrow bed.

II

You! – static, phrasic – narrow in a word
that's loaned by language and was imaged
to the manner born – *come, now, It Was Said!* –
did bleed into amendments magicked

all beyond, amazed, and minding tragic
outcomes undefined: Majestic in your hand –
or is that wrecked and ruined? – logic
the imperfect rhyme. We bound a wound?

We did. But no help from your wand.
Everyone could only look — not speak,
not write — and lean into the winter wind
that quickly left a salty film to reek

of sea spray upon every signaled E and K
of the *Ekstasis*. *Ekphrasis* stood by X and Y,
the way of things — standard method starts with A —
while *It Was Said* said only *Hi*, & then *Goodbye*.

First Fear

It's mechanical, they said, and I could make
The little monkey twist and somersault.
You'd wind it, tighten the spring with a key,
Looking at its cruel face. Then it did its tricks.

It whinged and whirred, and little arms flipped
It in the air. Three or four times it did this,
And then ran down. And then lay on its back.
I was told to pick it up, turn the key again.

The fur – is that what monkeys had? –
Was bristly to the point that it drew blood.
I was told to handle it gently. That I tried
To do, bristles sticking in my thumb.

This toy is the first gift I remember being given.
Please take it away, I begged.
It makes me scared. They all laughed and
Told me, *Wind it up again.* My Aunt,

Who had given me the gift, had a cruel face
And bristles on her chin. Down she stared at me.
Wind it up again, they said. *Watch the way it
Twists and turns those somersaults,*

Listen to it whinge and whine and whir.

Meeting Czesław Miłosz, 1984

I'd seen the posters for his lecture
As I arrived for my own, University
Of Michigan, 1984. All I thought
Was, so much for my audience.
But I was pleasantly surprised. I'd
Penciled in a quote from the Hass
Translation of a Miłosz poem, but
In the end didn't include it and stuck
With my text. I had nothing much
To say, in fact. After the polite applause,
I went to dinner with some young
Poets, drank too much wine, and then
To bed.
        Next morning, it occurred
To me that Miłosz must have been
Talking about *1984*. It was, after all,
1984, and Miłosz was political. Orwell
For some was still a kind of secular saint.
I wondered what the poet had said,
Was wondering as I opened the door
Of the guest house they'd put us in
And found myself staring at Miłosz
Himself, both of us with a toothbrush.
He looked – frightened. I suppose he
Was half asleep. As everyone in the
Guest house used the same communal
Bathroom, we were obliged to walk
Down the hall together with our
Toothbrushes and other toiletries.
Feeling that I needed to say something,
I mumbled: "How did your lecture go?
Sorry I couldn't make it." I could tell that
He too was trying to think of something
To say. "What were you doing?" he asked.

"I was giving a lecture. At the same
Time, but in a different building." He looked
At me – still seeming frightened – and said,
"Oh!" Or was it "O!"?
        No more than that. Years later
Hass wrote a poem in which Miłosz,
His great friend, asks from Kraków over
Long-distance telephone the difference
Between "O!" and "Oh!" Hass knew the
Answer, but back in 1984 I certainly didn't.
We both brushed our teeth in the same
Stained sink.
        Oh, sublime memories!
O, absurd mnemonics. I've just read Charles
Simic's review of the standard Miłosz
Biography. Oh, 1984! O, let all of us
Brush our teeth in peace.

A Balsa Wood Plane

A balsa wood plane would be one way
To get in the zone. These came in kits that
We'd find in the dime store for a dollar.
You'd assemble them quickly by fitting
The wing into a slot on the fuselage, the
Tail assembly likewise on the stern, and
Then you'd pinch a malleable weight
Onto the nose. It was ready, with small
Adjustments, to fly. We'd sail them off
The high bridge over Glen Echo Drive.
Sometimes in a good wind they'd sail
Far down the narrow road and turn
The corner as if actually maneuvered
By an imaginary pilot. Sometimes we
Never found the plane at all after we
Ran down the hill and around the bend.
It had left the glen for the zone, or found,
Where we couldn't yet see, just where
The ravine opened into the zone. It was
A while before we learned how to follow.

Acoustics Zones Shadows

(Pages of illustrations.)
— Wallace Stevens, 'Connoisseur of Chaos'

A zone full of acoustic shadows, or
A shadow full of zones. Such things,
Magister, are never one. They are not
Even two. Nor is place a zone, or zone
A place, nor do shadows offer shade.
Ages of nillustration, say, will take a
Child down the glen and leave him in
Dismay. He does not find the tables
From Connecticut where Englishmen
Had dined without their tea in Burma,
But sounds that have leapt at him from
Zones and zones from sounds
                                        that leapt
Like acrobatic dowsers, sounding space
With penises beyond their measure, paging
Through the zigzags where all pages
Dress Elizabethan, playing games. Gains
For peace at the pace of shadow, only
Echoing delay, deny perception of the war
Between a child and a man. The child
Is feather to the man, and only tickles him
When he should write. Night comes on.
Who's the buccaneer of chaos? Not the
Pensive man, not the natty connoisseur.

After Hölderlin

When I was a boy, he wrote,
I was rescued by gods from the world and
Punishments of men. In a glen full of echoes, warmed
By Helios, I escaped into a zone of oaks & elms,
Birds, brooks and cool winds, uncanny moments
Of poised silence and wellbeing. I was Endymion
Gazing upon splendor, catching sight of things
Eluding words, shapes moving in the woods,
Gestures of welcome made to me by presences
I came to love, which seemed at first to be nearby
But which, through the years, slowly drew away
And in the end wholly disappeared. When I became
A man I only had my memory to live by.

Glen Echo Business Men's Association

None of the businesses were in Glen Echo,
But as a name it had more resonance than
Hudson Street or Indianola, where most of
Them actually were. We'd come up out

Of the glen with sweaty faces and dirty hands
From an afternoon of looking for trouble along
The dry creek bed that led to the river that often
flooded well into the woods where

We built our fortified defenses and launched
Our canoe. No Glen Echo businessman knew
What we did, and though we laughed at them behind
Their counters and desks, eventually the

Tempting inventories brought us up out of
Danger and mischief. Don's Drugs had
Magazines and a soda bar; Haymaker's had
Toys and was called a "five and dime store";

And the "Homemade Delicatessen" had small
Blueberry pies you ate in your hand like
A sandwich. At a manually operated gate
For the level train crossing we'd share some

Peanuts from a large bag kept by the crossing
Guard who seemed to be a cranky old man but
Was friendly with kids, though not adults.
He'd raise and lower the gate for every crossing train

And stand there looking angry until it had passed.
Then he pulled up the gate and went back in his
Little shed by the tracks where some people said
He actually lived. Along with the large bags of

Peanuts and stacks of old papers he also had, to
Our surprise, a tall shelf of books. He said the books
Were mostly "dirty," but he shared the ones that
Weren't, saying "Still, don't tell your mom & dad."

Aside from my grandfather's vast Victorian library
In his old stone house on Iuka, the Train Man, as we
Called him (and he never told us his name) had
More books on his shelf than I had ever seen. His

Shed had a cozy and welcoming feel, especially in
Winter when he had a small coal fire in a grated
Stove with a tin chimney broken halfway off on
The tar-covered roof, but still functioning. There

Was a hot plate on the stove where he brewed
Coffee now and then. When I asked at home if
The Train Man was a member of the Glen Echo
Businessmen's Association, my father, mother, and

Aunt all laughed at once. What they didn't know
Was that Train Man was also the supplier of drugs to
Various down-and-outs. Nobody talked about drugs,
Though we all knew about drunks. Two old sisters

Were the only druggies we actually learned to
Recognize, standing together on the Glen Echo bridge with
Straggly hair and gazing into the zone we claimed
As our own in the actual glen. I borrowed books from

Train Man, the first I liked to read. Sometimes I'd sit
On the floor of his shed and talk about them. I had lots
Of questions. We both liked Howard Pease's adventure
Stories – mostly taking place on ships, but now and then

There would be one set on a train. There was *The Black
Tanker*, for instance, and *Singing Rails*. The tough old men
In those books and the kids they adopted had real business
To do. They'd head out at night and never come back.

A Leftie Friend & Mentor: After the McCarthy Years

I've only known one member of the American
Communist Party. He taught me history and life
At OSU. When it came to revolutions, he was
Wholly eloquent. He took off his glasses, took a deep

Breath, and dove into the past. It was as if he
Had himself been at the Bastille, and in the
Commune, and with Blanqui, *L'enfermé*. Back then
I was infirm, coming down with mononucleosis

In the middle of the term. Halfway up the stairs
In Non-capitulation Hall, I was unable to go on. I stopped
On a landing, gasping for breath. Late for days, I listened
By the classroom door, fevered, but taking it in. He

Was, I think, a great man. One of three I've known
In almost eighty years. I won't tell you his name in case
You rat on even posthumous profs. When he asked
me to dinner after I wrote a paper that he liked

I could hardly believe he thought I might
Be someone worth his time. He told me that a car
Arrived outside his house almost every morning.
Eventually, he and the CIA or FBI informant

Became friends. The man in the car was a former
Steel worker, and my teacher taught him to honor
The class he'd come from. In the end, the car stopped
Parking by his house. My mentor had stopped living there.

The agencies lost interest in his whereabouts. As for me,
I knew he was in Paris. I dedicated to him a short poem,
The first I ever published. My girlfriend – later on
My wife – stayed with me in his left bank hotel, the one where

Sartre and Beauvoir had lived a few years earlier.
Over breakfast, May of 1968, I joked: "You must have been
The only Commie living in Columbus, Ohio."
He said, "It was all perfectly legal. I was registered.

And also I was patriotic, believe it or not. The former
Steel worker who became my friend had earned an actual
Salary for sitting in his car all day outside my house.
After two years of doing this, he realized that it

Was not honorable work. He rejoined his union
And went back to making steel in Gary, Indiana.
It was, of course, the McCarthy era. His excuse, when
He offered one, was 'Pay no attention to my car.

I'm just a guy who needs to earn a decent wage.
I hope you understand.' That's when we had our little
Conversation. In those days, everybody did some
Unexpected thing. Stalin. Steel. We had to give up both,

You understand, in our benighted Middle West. I don't
Live there any longer, as you know. Sometimes former
Students like yourself arrive and visit. I enjoy that.
I liked the poem. I like your pretty girlfriend." I claimed,

Joking still, that I was a communist, like him. "Be a poet,"
He replied, "It's just as risky but a lot more fun. Look what
It's brought you already" – nodding toward Diana – "and you
didn't even have to sign a manifesto or petition."

I said: "*I'll* sign what *you* sign." "Not advisable," he said.
I said: "You live in Paris!" And he: "It's not by choice,
And you needn't be Jaurès to live here." He'd written
The biography of this hero and martyr for peace.

"My heart is breaking," said Anatole France, when
Jean Jaurès was shot. I quoted that. My friend shrugged:

"Be a poet," he repeated, "though I doubt you'll
Be much read. No one will murder you for poems."

He looked at me with a kind of generous pity in his eyes.
I knew he thought that I was too weak for barricades.
Outside, it was still May of 1968. We stayed inside.
I wrote a poem: "Aubade: For Diana in a Small Hotel."

What's Left on Iuka Drive

Mainly a few stones, but enough to remember
What there was. Even the arch over an artesian
Well and part of the wall around it have not wholly
Collapsed. We would sit on the wall, legs dangling
Down where we could see water at an uncertain
Depth, the big stone house behind us all full of
Old relations and even older "help," Fannie and
Annie, and an ancient retainer called Mr. Mann.
The house fell down a long time ago, but just
Discernable stairs still reach up from beside
The well to empty space at the top of the hill.
"What to play at Grandma's house?" we'd ask
Each other. The wittiest cousin said: "How about
We all play dead?" We might have played
September 19, 1862, but we didn't. The reason
Was that just like Generals Grant and Ord
We couldn't hear that a battle had already begun,
Suppressed as it was by an acoustic shadow.
All the dying happened in the old stone house,
But not one of us heard a single sound of
Lamentation and remorse.

Two Archives, Same Day

1

In the morning, it's the Ohio State Supreme Court.
I bring along a deposit, eight volumes of bound opinions
Written by Edward Shiloh and John Marshall Matthias,
Continuous without a break from 1915 to 1970 because
The latter succeeded the former in an unexpired term.
Two Justices and three librarians receive me. There is
Polite conversation, there are handshakes, there are small
Cups of coffee on a tray.

2

In the afternoon, I'm uptown at the OSU library asking
For the William Burroughs Papers. I was an undergraduate
Leftie and a would-be Beat from 1959 to 1963 when I
Hunted these stacks for contraband lit. Some of it had
Gotten publishers a day in court. I'm given boxes 17 and 18
After I've signed in and locked away my own stuff outside
The Department of Special Collections. The pretty librarian
Who brings me the boxes makes a joke about why I might be
Curious to read such "dated Hippie stuff." I tell her that
Mr. Burroughs was no Hippie, that it's all even more dated
Than that. Then I cautiously open the lids wondering what
Kind of contagion might lurk inside, if maggots might be
Crawling out of the moldering yellow manuscripts with
Marginalia by Ginsberg, Kerouac, and Burroughs himself.

3

Although I'm trying to be careful with my fingers
Fearing there might be a syringe between the papers

And the inside cardboard of the box, in fact I give
Myself a paper cut on the thumb. For a moment
I'm frightened, then rather thrilled. I've been cut
By the manuscript of *Naked Lunch*! Blood of my
Fathers from the Supreme Court! Should I ask for
A nurse? Word into my flesh. My blood on the word.
Feathers quill it somewhere in this killer hoard.

Unpublished Letter to the *New Yorker*
Professor Wisdom's Garden: A Prose Poem

I was surprised to read the parable attributed to Professor John Wisdom in James Wood's review, 'Unwelcome Guests,' ultimately about a book of stories by Joy Williams. But the first paragraph repeats a "theological parable" by Professor Wisdom that James Wood claims to have been "adapted and updated by others." That is to say, it seems to have become very well known, in various versions, by many thinkers. I fear that my friend, Igor Webb, and I may be responsible, as "unwelcome guests," for the original version. It is necessary to quote Mr. Wood.

> The version I first heard, years ago, went something like this: Two travellers return to a once neglected garden and find it miraculously restored to life. One of the travellers suggests that this is proof that a gardener has been tending the patch. The other disagrees, and they decide to set up watch. No one appears, which prompts the believer to suggest that an invisible gardener must be doing the work. Various monitors – bloodhounds, motion detectors, night-vision cameras – are put in place, but none register the appearance of the ghostly gardener. Finally, the skeptic asks the believer what meaningful difference there can be between a gardener who cannot be detected and a gardener who does not exist.

It happens that when we were graduate students at London University, 1966–67, we lived, for a very reasonable rent, in Professor Wisdom's house in Islington during the time when Wisdom was a visiting scholar at an American university. We took good care of the house, but entirely forgot that there was a walled garden in the back. Gradually, during our tenancy, it went to ruin. When we were made aware, only days in advance, of a pending visit from Professor Wisdom, we suddenly thought about the condition of the garden, opened one of the back windows, and looked at it hopelessly. We were able to hire someone to cut everything back, but there was nothing to do about the dead flowers, bushes, and — well, you know, though we did not, all the things that bloom in English gardens. Our mower kept murmuring to himself, "A bloody crime, a bloody crime," as he swung his scythe. We wonder if in some way or other we might be the source of the parable quoted in Wood's review. Perhaps there is indeed a meaningful difference between a gardener who cannot be detected and a gardener who does not exist. In the original version of the parable, we who did not detect a garden were undetected ourselves because inactive out of ignorance. In a later version, we were gardeners who did not exist. Or something like that. One must try to get these things straight.

A Note on Technology and Neighborhood

My plumber Jeff, who is also working across the street,
Tells me that our new neighbor is Kiera Duffy.
I say, "*The* Kiera Duffy?" He says, "I don't know – Kiera,
She's a singer." I say, "I know she's a singer; she's in
Fact a *famous* singer." Jeff goes back across the street.
Me, I get on the computer and visit iTunes. I order up
Kiera Duffy's *Strauss Songs,* wait a few minutes, and
Then listen in. She sings from the small speakers in
My MacBook. Soon enough, the download reloads
Itself into my Sonos system. Now she sings all over
The house through eight speakers in various rooms.
Not content with a disembodied voice, I check out
YouTube, where I find her singing Handel. She is
A beautiful singer (and a lovely woman as well, as
I now can see.) I also remember that she's singing
This week in Berlin with the Philharmonic, and that
I subscribe to the direct feed. But why has she
Come to South Bend? Shouldn't she live in Paris
Or New York or, for that matter, Berlin? Same reason,
I guess, that I came to the university here: for a job,
Health insurance, benefits, and retirement pay
(On which, at the moment, I survive). The voice, alas,
Does eventually age.
                                   Just here I put this poem
On hold and await developments. Very early Thursday
A taxi arrives across the street. It's still dark out, but
I'm wide awake and reading a book by Alex Ross.
I look out the window and see a bundled-up woman
(It must be Kiera) getting into the cab. It's January and
It's very cold outside. I assume she has an early flight
To Berlin. Once again I put down the poem and wait
Until Saturday, now. This *now* is "real time." I click on the
Digital Concert Hall and find the orchestra in place.
In comes the conductor; in comes Kiera Duffy to

Sing some Ravel. They all look delighted to be there.
I'm delighted to be there too, or rather delighted to
Be here looking at *there* in real time. Hello Kiera.
Hello Simon Rattle, hello first violinist tuning on A.
They begin. I look across the street and see in the window
Her husband — also a singer, says Jeff — with their child.
He bounces the child on his knee and leans forward
To do something. He's adjusting the volume, just as
I am, while still bouncing the child on his knee. I
Think he must like Ravel. I'm sure he likes his wife's
Voice. Do we think the same thing? Here's transcendent
Music that through all of us lives for a moment by
Technology and neighborhood. Alex Ross, are you
Watching this as well? If so, from where? His book
Is called *Listen to This*. Well, we're all listening.
Meanwhile, Jeff has repaired the plumbing in both
The house across the street and our own. Things
For a moment seem more right than wrong.
When Kiera returns, I think I'll introduce myself.

Priest Hole

It's something like that, and I lived there
For a while when they told me I was ill.
What did they do, the priests, hidden by
The secret Catholics in those dark places
In the years when religious wars raged
Everywhere? At Notre Dame, the one in
Indiana, priests walk freely, teach theology,
Serve as deans and provosts. But it was
There where I went underground. I wrote from
The interstices of walls, disappearing in the
Night into wet clay that might have been
A deep trench from the First World War.
A priest hole. Many times I'd visited the
Castles at Framlingham and Orford, now
Tourist sites near my wife's Suffolk home in
Hacheston. At one of them, Mary Tudor got
The word that she was queen. Many priests
Popped up all over England. Me, I stayed
In my hole even when news seemed favorable.
I was just a poet, and no one representing me
And my kind would suddenly be queen.

Another Fall

Once again he had fallen down. He was
Getting good at it. He had fallen off a ferry pier
Into the Adriatic near Dubrovnik. He had
Fallen over the wall around Central Park
Through the limbs of a large tree. Had it not
Been for the sea in one case, and the limbs
Of the tree in the other, he would have suffered
Grievous wounds. Does one say "grievous wounds"
Anymore? That would give it too much dignity,
Make it sound like something honorable — say, for
Example, the injury his great-grandfather suffered
When a Rebel musket ball shattered his elbow
In the Civil War . . . .
                              As for our citizen,
Our man, our mensch — O poor bonhomme —
He merely slipped and fell on the icy steps of
His own house. There was no warm sea
Or kind branch to cushion his dive. It was
Chaplinesque, Monsieur Poirot in a pratfall.
Did his head burst like a Halloween pumpkin?
People passing in a car laughed at first; it looked
So like an acrobatic trick that they hadn't a clue
He'd suffered a grievous wound. Come and help him
Someone. This is not a joke. This is not Halloween.

Changing Your Seat

for Michael

> *. . . and in*
that awkward moment, leaning slightly forward
sliding your feet sideways so that you wouldn't

step on the toes of people whose fronts your back
was brushing against – "pardon me," "excuse me" –
you find an empty seat and sit down. But just as you

start getting into the film, the person directly behind
you starts to cough and sneeze. Jeez, you think, it's the
middle of winter and the guy's got the flu. You'd better

change your seat, except you don't see an empty one
on your row and when the guy coughs again you start
getting embarrassed because the girl and boy to your left

start making out just as if they were alone in their car
and not in a crowded movie theatre – a movie "Palace" in fact –
where the architecture is wholly baroque and, as they'd say

in later decades, "totally over the top," although what tops
all of this off is the fact that the guy on your right
has put his hand in your crotch, and you think – in fact

you actually *say* – "I'm not going to sit here with
some stranger grabbing my crotch, I'm going to
change my seat," and then you don't just *say*, you stand

up and *shout*, "Usher, get me out of this row and away
from all this sex and disease! That stuff's just for the movies,
not for my actual life, and I'm only fifteen and

scared and alone in this dark and palatial place
that is passing strange and into which I seem to be lodged
like a wholly illegible word in a lewd and ludic ledger."

Yet Another Typo

> ". . . and among other things, he was
> the most distinguished hair of Wallace Stevens."

We suppose the author means *heir*, but why
Not let it stand. Even Stevens, we suppose,
Had bad hair days, and might have once or twice
Personified both the good and the bad coifs.
But to be "the most distinguished" of all, what
An honor. I look at him perched on the head
Of the famous portrait of Stevens on the jacket
Of the expensive hardback of *Collected Poems*.
But I have to say that even here the hair is not
Quite perfect. A breath of wind seems to have
Flipped a little lock toward the back of his head
So that it stands up almost straight. The photographer
Should have seen that, and offered him a comb.

Ashbury

is a small village in England,
not far from Mortmere, and both are
all but hidden in the fens. There is
little recorded history of either place,
but it is rumored that a butcher
from Ashbury once stole a pig
from a Mortmere farm. Women mostly
stay indoors, while those who work
the land would rather sit for their likeness
when the portrait painter comes, although
this happens only once in a generation.
In Cambridge, only very few have ever
been to either village, and those who
have divide into narrow factions. Fictions
thrive in both, of course, so visitors are
warned away by signs: Not as you'd suppose
saying *Stay Out*, but surprisingly *Come In*.

There Was a Plan

There was a plan, just a very few
Years back, that Peter and Michael
And I would indulge in Sixties nostalgia
And give together a reading in Boulder,
Then pour libations on Ed Dorn's grave.
All too soon Peter had a stroke and
Michael phoned to tell me of his own
Grim diagnosis. And me — I just
Got tired, very tired. They had intended
To film our reading, the university
Had said, in memory of times long gone.
When I first met Peter he was still
Fresh from Big Daddy Lipscomb's forearm
Shiver in a pro ball tryout and about to sing
The first *Pacific Plainsong*, while Michael
In a second-hand elegy imagined driving
Downtown in Dayton, Ohio, where
My uncle Richard ran a department store
And drank more than even my father,
"Waiting for something to happen."

Barkan Classic Merlot

i.m., Joel Barkan, and for Sandy

What do you do when your oldest
friend suddenly disappears from the earth? –
(Mexico, aneurism, local cremation.) I get
a call when it's all happened and his
wife – hard to think "widow" – weeping
over the phone just says, "Joel suddenly
died." What you do is go to a small
Italian grocery near your home and buy
a bottle of Barkan Classic Merlot –
bottled by Barkan Wine Cellars, Ltd.
in Galil, Israel. You take it with you to
Merrimans' Playhouse, a very 1950s
jazz club in South Bend, Indiana, where
you've lived for much longer than you
would have expected. You tell Steve
that you haven't read poetry to jazz
since 1959, when it was a fad to do
this and when you and Joel, when he
played bass in a trio, used to imitate
Rexroth, Ferlinghetti, and the cool
cats in San Francisco trying to find
the right way to do this wrong kind
of thing. Steve's sympathetic, and we
uncork the bottle of Barkan Classic Merlot.
I pour a small libation onto the floor
where Steve's dog, Charlie Barker, licks
it up. The rest we divide among the guys
in the band. We toast the dead and the
living. I try to read a poem I wrote in
high school, the first thing I really thought
might be good. Somehow I get through it.
I thank Steve and the band, go out into
the night and drive home. Then I write

this poem for Sandy. She'll know the
chronology is more than a little off because
it's now been years since Joel's death.
But never mind. I had no idea what to do
when he died. But then, tonight – how strange –
I suddenly did.

Coal and Ice

What did I know, what did I know?
—Robert Hayden, "Those Winter Sundays"

We had an icebox and a coal bin. It was
that long ago. The iceman came and also
the coal man — in good time, in good time.
The iceman used to give me a sliver of
his block, saying *this will melt, this will
melt — but suck on it as if it were your
mother's tit.* The coal man said, *I send
the earth's black magic down your
chute, where you will find it on the
coldest February days. It won't mean
much in August when you want to
suck on ice. But when the whole world
is ice in winter, you'll remember me.*

Dr. Hemo

In my wife's Parkinson's group, all of them
Groping at almost impossible movements,
The man bent absolutely double, the worst
At all maneuvers to outsmart deficiency of
Dopamine in the *substantia nigra*, was once
The best hematologist in the Midwest, and the
Man who saved my life. It took me half an hour
To see that he was there among the afflicted, my
Attention all devoted to my wife whose movements,
I'm told by the therapist after the session, are
Among the best. I'm proud of her. But what of
Dr. Hemo, as I used to call him when I'd complain
About the poison in my blood? (My wife's doctor
We of course call Dr. Neuro.) Trying to unbend,
Holding with a hand to one of two rings in the gym
That athletes swing themselves so high on that
They look like angels in the sky, he notices my
Glance. Or does not. Involuntarily I mouth out
Thank you. And then I think: *fly, fly, fly.*

Like William Carlos Williams

in Rutherford, New Jersey, have I
come to love my neighbors even more
than the international avant-garde?
I never expected this to happen.
Certainly not in South Bend, Indiana.
Though I've lived here for fifty years,
it was always a deep embarrassment to
hear about the "Hoosiers." And now our
former governor, Theocrat of a primitive kind,
is first in line to replace the Emperor Trump.
"Great-Jill-o'-the-Tump-that-bare-me," David
Jones intoned, leaning toward his Welshness,
praying for every Jac o' the Tump in need:
"Save us, Tellus of the myriad names, from
the Ram's curia." Curious, that. And he with his
thumb still in *Finnegans Wake* . . . I came
here from London via San Francisco, Palo Alto,
(never mind about Columbus, Ohio before that:
a *Buckeye* for your *Hoosier,* Mr. Kurtz).
Cosmopolitan. International.
But here I worked
at a job; here my children were born; here I'll
be buried, I suppose, or burned. Do I love
my neighbors as myself? Not quite, but I like
them more than I used to. Would I lie
with them, would I scatter myself in their
flower beds? I'm told that the family
plot in nearby Columbus – now a
full-fledged city – is "pretty full." But that's
all right with me. I never got on with
all my Republican cousins and would
just as soon spend eternity beside a
few English professors from Notre Dame.
That is, if they agree to give me a place

in the Catholic graveyard or a slot in the wall
where alums can pay their way if they're
not expecting resurrection of the flesh but
just forever after in a box full of ash. Today I go
neither to earth nor ash, but just The Law.
My superstition tells me that once I've
signed my name to certain documents, what
they prophecy will soon come true. Hail *Logos,*
or perhaps *Davhar.* Something in me always
wanted to be Jewish like my best friends down
the years – Joel Barkan, V. I. Wexner, Peter
Michelson. My friend Tony Kerrigan obtained
a Notre Dame grave, in spite of being a bigamist.
And Joe Duffy, everyone knows, was hardly
a communicant. Among the last of my generation,
I think of all those clever pals who checked
the "Catholic" box hoping for early tenure.
Me, I'd rather have a tenor bellowing either
Hebrew or Latin, languages more dignified than
our ruined American English. Dear W. C. W.,
had you only known. You said a poem could be
made out of anything, even a grocery list.
But have a look – a listen – to what is now
said in the store. It might send you to Europe
out of despair, like Ez. Me, I've been there, and
it's too late to go back. Any lack of dignity's by
now okay. I'll sign where it says "sign." I've got
no ancient laurels on my Middle Western brow.

From a Place in Tübingen

Pears and wild roses and a good land
Hanging over the lake when
Swans dipped their heads as sacrament
Into the crystal summer water.

But, alas, not now. Where can I find
The rose or pear or sunshine in this
Winter of my mind, this winter of asylum
Where I live assailed on every side.

Inside and outside walls of stone and
Bone, strange flags jangle on their poles,
Flap and flutter in the heavy wind.

After Hölderlin: his last poem

For Peter Robinson, Dentist

In the old days, everyone's teeth fell out
By a certain age — an age, in fact, that both
Of us passed some years ago. But thanks
To modern dentistry, we both chew on.
Chew on, chow down! It will doubtless be
Antibiotics that fail us, once we swallow
Some kind of contaminated frozen dinner
Waiting too long on the freezer shelf.

I understand that skulls with teeth are
Much prized by anthropologists. I have no
Intention of leaving one behind — the fire
For me — and may it not leave a tooth!
But I've had actual friends whose skulls
And teeth I know are on somebody's office
Desk. Can they be a *memento mori* and
At the same time an exhibit of good dental
Hygiene? All those slides your father kept
on your dining room table — they'd gross
me out, as I've mentioned in other poems.
He was an oral pathologist, teaching students
From intimate pictures of people who'd
Died from their lesions, almost, I thought,
A kind of oral pornography. But no one
Would really want even the best kind
Of blowjob from any mouth like these!
We've talked a lot about the things you say
We "used to get up to." Going down the ravine,
We'd look for trouble and sometimes find
More than we could handle — like the naked man,
Disturbed by us while fucking a girl in his car,
Who chased us half a mile yelling and screaming.
He still appears in my dreams. I've told friends
That, at Walter Reed, you "worked on" Eisenhower

And Omar Bradley. Those who remember the
Names at all always ask: "On their teeth?" Well,
I've told them, maybe just their gums. On the
Other hand, maybe you saved their actual teeth.
I'm not sure. And maybe their skulls are themselves
Both *memento mori* and examples of dental hygiene.
I can hear the lecturer saying, pointing to them
On his desk: "Gentlemen, these are the actual teeth
Of Dwight D. Eisenhower and General Omar Bradley.
Think how they all lasted through those wars!
With the Normandy invasion just a few days off,
No one in the world wanted to hear either one of
Them say: 'Call it all off. I've got this awful toothache,
And I can't think about anything else.'" At present
All of my own teeth are okay, though one's an implant
And many others are crowned. Luckily, I don't
Need to go chase Nazis from the beachhead to Berlin,
But I still chase life. How long can we do that,
Putting our teeth on edge, as the saying goes? Do
I have still a sweet tooth for certain things despite
My root canals? Do you? You're the only friend
I've got left from my old neighborhood, my pal
With whom I went down into the magical zone
We simply called "the ravine." That naked man
Would have given us much worse than a bite.
He was out to kill us both. He was death itself.
Somehow, we knew that, and somehow got away.

DVD Transfer

In the old days everyone watching the first
Home movies, jerking around the reels
And exposing frames to the light, would often
Shout – *There's Aunt Jean, there's Uncle Jim,*
There's Grandma Crouch, there's The Judge,
There's Lois, there's Johnny. When I had
The old films transferred to DVD, I took the disc
To Columbus and managed to get Lois, my mother,
Into a public space cleared for private use
Where we could show the new disc on a large
Screen, hoping for clarity. *Who's that?* she asked.
That's Aunt Jean, your sister Jean, and that's
Me, you, father. *Who?* she asked. *Never saw those*
People in my life. Why are they so big? Will you
Turn them off? You're making me scared.

Octaves

Fangled bitch, my Age, who will ever gaze
into your wolfish pisspot face?
Whose blood the glue to stick your backbones
back together after a millennium?
Maker's blood splashes from an old passport
into mug of whore Age's desperate case.
On prison sills of grim future's coin, spends
a hanging man his comfort's lot.

*

Cannot stop the blood maker's flood
from gushing into everything that lives and dies,
ill-ebbed of floodtides, tossing fire-fish
on the sea-bone sodden sand,
while above it all the netted songbirds bride-
sing the sorrow as it pours and pours,
fangled bitch, my Age,
upon your wounded living dying hide.

After Mandelstam, 'The Age'

II

Some Zones

I grew up thinking a good deal about "zones." When I was very young, the war was still on, so the radio was always talking about the war zone – one in Europe, another in the Pacific. As my father was a municipal court judge, there was talk at home about crime scenes that also occurred in zones that you could see identified in maps of the city, which happened to be Columbus, Ohio. After the war, Berlin had an Allied Zone and a Soviet Zone. People were not yet said to be "zoned out," but that would come later. One also heard of "disaster zones," though they always seemed far away. My pals and I referred to zones down in the Glen Echo ravine, where we played together, sometimes from dawn to dusk. There was a "brain zone" and a "bone zone," bone being short for bonehead. We always stayed as far away from the toughs of the bone zone as possible, since it was controlled by the thuggish kids who lived down the alley and always wanted to start fights. In our "brain zone," we made up elaborate imaginative games with costumes and props. We also managed to make verbal play and anagrams out of the word: "One Z" (for a bad night's sleep); "Eonz' (for Eons), and of course Zeno (him with the arrow). We often carried arrows ourselves (and bows to shoot them with), and sometimes BB guns. These were for protection lest we strayed over the ambiguous borders, badly drawn through woods and over hills, into the bone zone and had to defend ourselves.

As we grew older, we imagined zones in the city for which we were personally responsible. There was a "Barkan zone," which, as Joel Barkan's father was a professor, was mainly in the area around Ohio State University; the "Matthias zone" had two sectors: the deep ravine area on the north side, and, via the Olentangy River fed by Glen Echo Creek, all the way downtown to the city center. The "Goss zone" was on the west side of town where new suburbs bordered the Franklin County countryside from which Conestoga wagons once headed to California.

During this adolescent period, I became obsessed with time zones. If we drove or took the train west, I was convinced that I was actually growing younger. When travel by plane became commonplace, I realized that in some longer flights I could arrive before I took off. My first form of entertainment was the radio, not TV, and I was once myself on a program called *The Story Hour*. The soundproofed studio with sound engineers behind glass windows staring down at our table full of microphones was entirely out of this world. It was a nationally aired program, and I realized that it was three hours earlier in California and so I was broadcasting into the future. When we finally got a TV, one of the most popular shows of the period was Rod Serling's *The Twilight Zone.* Serling had attended Antioch College, which was an avant-garde kind of institution a short distance from Columbus where Barkan, David Goss, and I attended jazz concerts and plays, including one of the first U.S. performances of *Waiting for Godot.* I had a serious girlfriend at Antioch – unusual in those days, and especially so given she was two years older – who was a French major. One day she showed me a translation of Apollinaire's 'Zone.' His zone was Paris, but I conjured Columbus out of it anyway, going on eventually to co-translate with my hyper-advanced lady friend parts of Rimbaud's 'Drunken Boat' into our own muddy river, rowing

Via *New Directions* and starting on the Olentangy,
On my local river, Huck, and it was where it flowed
Beside the stadium for football and within a bend
Or two the stone State House where my own father

Was *juge* (a judge) as the categories morphed
If not the work itself by just a bit through all the
Vowels: a black *a* / a white *e* / a red *i* / a green *u* /
A blue *a* / and therefore I was RED and that was

Just the trouble, *Juge*, when I thought the rest were
Yellow as in *cowards* with the jaundice and so
Utterly unzoned . . .

Our boat, actually a canoe, could be launched from the creek into the river and sailed, we hoped, in the general direction of Apollinaire's muse, *Bergère ô tour Eiffel le troupeau des ponts bêle ce matin!*

It was a strange and sometimes risky journey from the Glen Echo ravine all the way downtown past city hall and into that part of my own zone that included not only civic buildings, movie theatres, and old-fashioned department stores, but also that part of the town that really beckoned to us, the African American neighborhoods ("Negro streets," we called them, echoing Ginsberg's *Howl*) where we had discovered Marty's 502, a jazz club, where we were the only white and also the only underage regulars. There we saw and heard Monk and Miles, Trane and Blakey, Silver and Roach – and many others. Was this a zone within a zone? We had difficulty with the idea of "place," a word introduced by the very practical Goss. "Isn't a place the same as a zone?" he'd ask. Barkan would say, "It's the opposite of a zone, you goof." As for me, I wasn't sure. In the same way that my father's "crime scenes" were established within zones determined by "zoning laws," so our places, groovy ones like Marty's 502, also occurred in zones – in my own zone, actually. Marty's was a very real "place," and you could direct anybody to it if they asked you. But Marty's was also in a zone – and maybe even a zone unto itself. These things were difficult. Did we hear Monk's music in a place within a zone, a zone within a place, or a zone within a zone? I am still unable to decide. If Barkan was right and a zone was the *opposite* of a place, I had some thinking to do.

Meanwhile, the BB gun wars we had started in the Glen Echo ravine came to the attention of the Columbus police. The bone zone thugs had challenged us and we agreed to a fight. Rules were strict. No aiming above the shoulders. Many on both sides wore football helmets and sunglasses for protection. Nonetheless, Michael Mersky was shot in the eye, having brought along his gun but not his helmet or glasses. His parents called the police and we were all interviewed. Michael spent an afternoon in the OSU hospital. We all thought he'd look great with an eye patch. As it turned out, the BB was lodged in the white of his eye, and was easily extracted. We were all disappointed, hoping for a brain zone martyr of some kind, and went back to Barkan's place after we got the news. It was time to watch *The Twilight Zone*.

It was now October 1959. We didn't know that William Burroughs had just published his *Naked Lunch* in Apollinaire's Paris zone with Olympia Press. Nor that Paul Carroll would go to court for trying to print excerpts in the *Chicago Review* and found *Big Table* in order to do so. I had notes from teachers allowing me to visit the OSU library and take out *Howl* and *Tropic of Cancer. Howl* was dedicated to, inter alia, "William Seward Burroughs, author of *Naked Lunch*, an endless novel which will drive everyone mad." It appeared to have something to do with drugs, which the author called "Junk." But we weren't yet there. Dave and Joel and I took turns reading *Howl* aloud and finding passages in Miller's *Tropic* that we thought would shock the girls in our class. Maybe the *Tropic* was a zone. But it was not *about* a zone. Paris in the *Tropic* was a place, unlike Paris in Apollinaire. The *Lunch* was served up in a zone, but for a while we didn't get the distinction because we hadn't read the book. Still, Antioch College's Rod Serling gave us more than a hint of where we were headed.

It's hard to remember now how famous Serling was in those days. Squares went home to watch *I Love Lucy,* while *The Twilight Zone* was for the hip and cool. But was "the Lucy show" a zone? To those of us zoning in the twilight, it was the kind of place that Barkan called the opposite of a zone. And yet the bus driver, Jackie Gleason, could have slipped, incognito, into almost any of Serling's scripts. Gleason, later "Minnesota Fats" in a cinematic pool hall duel with Paul Newman, could have done a cameo in *The Twilight Zone* or even *Naked Lunch*. Every girl and gay man in America lusted after Newman. Gleason would have been his antitype in any zone and both, in fact, might have appeared zoned in or out of our contemporary Serling-like *Westworld*, whether as guests or hosts.

I think we must have missed "Where Is Everybody," which was the pilot of *The Twilight Zone*. Looking back at the half-hour episode that began the TV series that is still something of a cult favorite, I can see that it's an allegory about loneliness. It is nearly ruined at the end, however, by an explanation of its otherwise brilliant examination of a town where everything is working but where no human being can be found, by positing a medical-psychological experiment undertaken by the military on a volunteer who awakens from a chemically induced dream. The medical officer says: "there's one thing we can't simulate, and that's a very basic need. Man's hunger for companionship. That's a barrier we don't know how to breach yet. The barrier of loneliness." But no true zone is allegorical. A zone is what it is. Maybe Barkan was right. Serling in his pilot episode ruined his zone by naturalizing and explaining it as a place — the military experiment and its setting. No true zone can be explained.

By October 30, 1959, Serling was quickly getting better. The half hour of "Walking Distance" is a kind of domestic-American version of Tarkovsky's *Stalker* (to which film we will eventually come). The twilight zone on this walker's plod is his native town and his childhood where his adult self is not recognized, even by his own parents. Everything about 1950s America is jolted back to the narrator's 1930s childhood in a "symphony of summer."

> There was a pavilion with the big, round, band-concert stand. There was the merry-go-round, loaded with kids, the brassy, discordant calliope music still chasing it round and round. There were the same wooden horses, the same brass rings, the same ice-cream stands, cotton candy vendors. And always the children. Short pants and Mickey Mouse shirts. Lollipops and ice-cream cones and laughter and giggling. The language of the young . . . . The sounds swirled around him. Calliope, laughter, children. Again the right feeling in his throat. Bittersweet again. All of it had been left so far behind and now he was close to it.

When the narrator's father fails to recognize him he says earnestly, "I just wanted to tell you what's going to happen." His father doesn't want to hear. He says, "I don't want it to be a dream." And this time it is not, it is a zone. "I just don't want time to pass, do you understand? I want it to be the way it is now."

Within a few months, all of America knew Serling's voice, which spoke, in this instance, before the conventional "fade to black":

> *And like all men perhaps there'll be an occasion, maybe a summer night sometime, when he'll look up from what*

he's doing and listen to the distant music of a calliope —
and hear the voices and the laughter of the people and the
places of his past. And perhaps across his mind there'll flit
a little errant wish — that of his youth. And he'll smile then
too because he'll know it is just an errant wish. Some wisps
of memory, some ghosts that cross a man's mind . . . that
are a part of The Twilight Zone . . .

I am in fact quoting this from a book I have in hand edited by Rod Serling's daughter, *Stories from the Twilight Zone.* In her foreword, Anne Serling quotes one of the original actors, Don Gordon, saying that the show "had that quality that radio used to have before television." Fifty-eight years after watching the first season of *Twilight Zone* episodes, I find Gordon's remark fascinating. My generation was the *only* generation in America that made a transition from listening exclusively to watching early TV. I remember listening to programs intended for adults like *G.E. Theater, Dangerous Assignment, Alfred Hitchcock Presents*, and many others. My bedroom lights were out. Voices whispered from the face of a green-glowing contraption saying things I often didn't understand, like the enigmatic codes that Jean Cocteau's Orpheus hears on his car radio in the movie *Orphée.* Whatever I made of it was as much the result of my own half-awake imagination as it was that of the interacting intentions of some far-off group of radio actors, directors, and writers. And that is exactly what Don Gordon goes on to say: "Your imagination is allowed to work on *Twilight Zone.* You're invited in — to think. They're not bombarding you and saying 'you're stupid, we're going to tell you what this is all about.' You're a participant, and that's very important." LeRoi Jones (not yet Amiri Baraka) knew what Don Gordon meant when he wrote 'In Memory of the Radio':

Who has ever stopped to think of the divinity of Lamont
        Cranston?
(Only Jack Kerouac, that I know of, & me.
The rest of you probably had on WCBS and Kate Smith . . .
"Who knows what evil lurks in the hearts of men? The
        Shadow knows!"

O, yes he does
O, yes he does

This poem, too, available to Donald Allen for *The New American Poetry*, put together in that same magical year of 1959, was written with the Sixties just in view. Lamont Cranston? He was himself "The Shadow," spooking me in Frank Readick's scary voice. Try the Wikipedia zone, which leaks the following (correct) information:

> The introduction from *The Shadow* radio program "Who knows what evil lurks in the hearts of men? The Shadow knows!" usually spoken by actor Frank Readick Jr., has earned a place in the American idiom. These words were accompanied by an anonymous laugh and a musical theme, Camille Saint-Saëns' *Le Rouet d'Omphale* ('Omphale's Spinning Wheel,' composed in 1872). At the end of each episode The Shadow reminded listeners that, "The weed of crime bears bitter fruit. Crime does not pay . . . The Shadow knows!"

Because the Barkan zone extended into the OSU campus, we knew about the Hays Hall Wednesday afternoon art film series. There we saw, surrounded by authentic film buffs, early work by Bergman, Antonioni, Fellini, and − among his younger contemporaries − the old modernist Jean Cocteau. *Orphée* was a great hit among us, especially the several scenes of radio broadcasts. These were clearly coming from a zone beyond any that we, or Orpheus himself, had formerly had access to. We didn't know, of course, that the repeated encryptions were lines of Cocteau's own poems, or that he was referencing actual transmissions during World War II from London to the Resistance in France − a war zone, of course, but also a place where a radio operator might dial in a frequency broadcasting in cypher to the likes of René Char, both directing his activities as a member of the Resistance and providing material which, as Carrie Noland writes in *Poetry at Stake: The Aesthetics and Challenge of Technology*, was used to make verbal artifacts using "the historically saturated discourse of the radio. A reading of

Char's poetry through contemporaneous discourses on – and of – the radio, suggests that the very technological apparatus Heidegger taxes with distancing poetry from the truth . . . promises, for Char, truth's conveyance and preservation."

Ignorant of both Char and Heidegger, all we knew was that Orpheus was being summoned to a zone that was the underworld. Whether or not zones were actually under anything, they were deeply *elsewhere*, even those of which we remained in charge, where familiar things were made strange or strange things made familiar. But it made metaphorical sense to think of them as netherworlds like the one discovered by Alice, tumbling down the rabbit hole. We didn't yet know Dante or Virgil, but we did know that a descent could be horizontal as well as vertical. Alice could be found at Marty's 502 Club, but we were the only people who knew it. If they broadcast Monk or Miles on the right frequency, someone in the *maquis'* ghostly southern zone in, let us say, Toulouse, might gather yet for a moonlight drop on orders from De Gaulle. The right music was both muse and mischief, bending codes of *Messages Personnels,* those BBC messages to France, into Char's *Hypnos Leaves,* and poems possibly declaring "*l'adoration des bergers n'est plus utile à la planète.*"

Our fathers had not fought in the war and, perhaps for that very reason, we found the few survivors that we knew almost mythological figures, as if they had fought at Troy rather than in France. But France was good enough. Especially France. A modest neighbor of mine had survived both the Normandy landings and the Battle of the Bulge. When it became known that J.D. Salinger had managed to visit Ernest Hemingway in an active battle zone, our veteran simply shrugged and said, "Things like that happened all the time." I couldn't think of any other "things like that," but never mind. A zone was a zone was a zone.

The adoration of shepherds was no longer useful; "*l'adoration des bergers n'est plus utile à la planète.*" One major question was whether or not zones – where shepherds abided or costumed kids played games – had anything to do with utility. By the time we had access to the Paris edition of *Naked Lunch* – Barkan's older brother brought it back from a holiday[1] – we were thinking that the true zones were intersections of gratuitous desire and a playable space. Burroughs' "Interzone" in *Naked Lunch* seemed to be a version of the International Zone in Tangiers, but also a dystopian version of a political state with Swiftian big- and small-endians called Liquefactionists, Senders, Factualists, and Divisionists. Beyond that, the Interzone offered appalling orgies presided over by sadists in their unique form of play. Although we may have been the first in our town to read William Burroughs, we didn't know what to make of *Naked Lunch*. Good vibes or bad? Utopian zones displaced by dystopian obscenities? Or was dystopian obscenity itself a language of access to some super-reality?

But use? The *utile?* Many years later I became a serious reader of the works of David Jones, best known for the experimental *In Parenthesis* (1937) based on his experiences during the First World War. In that book, the phantasmagoric region of the trench system itself is a kind of zone, but David Jones' later reconfiguration of it in the *The Book of Balaam's Ass*, basically a draft of passages that never found a place in *The Anathémata*, Jones' second book-length poem from 1952, are in some ways analogous to Burroughs' Interzone and, like it, a malign space, but verbally remarkable.

In our *Twilight Zone* phase, we had assumed a neutral position with regard to the fundamental question of utility vs. gratuity. We eventually speculated a bit about whether or not gratuity itself could achieve utility. Does the gratuitous world of play in fact prepare one for practical tasks? Far from us in London, Wales, and Palestine of the British Mandate, David Jones thought not. The entire world of utility confronted gratuity's desire to praise and play with obstacles almost beyond the imagination of William Burroughs. In *The Book of Balaam's Ass*, David Jones imagines a zone based on the military camp near Winchester where the author was stationed before embarking for France and the trenches of *In Parenthesis*. This zone is identified as utility's apotheosis. Nothing exists for itself; everything exists for the sake of what it can do, or what it can make people do. It took me until 1966 to become aware of David Jones, but it

---

[1] The "fact" is that Joel Barkan had no older brother. Nonetheless, he brought back the French edition of *Naked Lunch* from a visit to Paris.

moves me now to think about him writing his brilliant texts while I thought about Burroughs and Serling exploring zones, which Jones had foreseen in such an unusual way. It was also around 1966 that the Ohio State library began receiving deposits that have become one of the most important William Burroughs archives in the world. (This in puritanical, philistine Columbus, Ohio.) There in the old Barkan zone one can read the 1959 typescript of *Naked Lunch* that was used for the French Olympia edition and long thought to have been lost. From this and other holdings it became clear that one title considered for the book as a whole had indeed been *Interzone*.

Naked Lunch was a slowly accumulating and even haphazard affair. So were those fragments of David Jones' writings gathered after his death as *The Roman Quarry*, which included *The Book of Balaam's Ass*. With both books early quasi-collaborators, friends, and later editors put together fragments that, although they may not entirely cohere, contain passages that are brilliant.

The moment of greatest significance in *Balaam's Ass* occurs following a set of asterisks appearing just after the passage excerpted in Jones' *The Sleeping Lord and Other Fragments* of 1966. In fact, new material in *The Sleeping Lord* is framed by two modified passages from *Balaam's Ass*. This is from the original manuscript:

> I've known him to cut a square stone in the South wall . . . others he quarries in Tooting Bec . . . The Zone is his great problem – you can't say much about the Zone. We all know the Zone, we all weep in the Zone . . . they beat his messengers in the Zone. He's naked in the Zone . . . If you went to the Zone to curse you might manage it . . . It's always 3 p.m. in the Zone. All the doors are shut in the Zone. All roads intersect in the Zone. He's emptied the Zone of Being by an incredibly complicated process . . .

"He" in this passage is *not*, as it frequently is in colloquial Tommy references to the enemy as "he" ("against whom we found ourselves by misadventure") of *In Parenthesis*, an acknowledgment of a kind of brotherhood. "He" seems to be universal "authority" as sheer instrumentality, an omnipotence bending everything to use, even though his messengers are beaten and the Zone is a great problem for him. Emptying the zone of Being, shutting all doors, plotting all roads to intersect, he sees to it that it is always three in the afternoon, the hour of Christ's death. He purges man's inherent nature to play and praise, to make and recognize the gratuitous signs of art. There is no shadow in the Zone, no recession, nothing beyond a single plane; it's a place where all life is a matter of conditioning, where he has found a common denominator for all his "devices," where no one complains. "It would be difficult," the speaker maintains, "to think meanly of King Pellam's Land, but what shall we say of this place?"

In *In Parenthesis*, superimposed upon the phantasmagoria of the First World War trench system, was in fact King Pellam's Land, the Arthurian waste land also evoked in T.S. Eliot's poem of 1922, but in David Jones much more comprehensively and successfully. The war zone in *In Parenthesis* was also a zone of human complexity, desire, intentionality, artistic making, and prayer. But the Zone on the heath denies all of these things, and the false prophetess, Mrs. Balaam, is told that "after a long burden of prophecy," she might go to the Zone as if to the source of all evil and error.

At this point the narrator, finally in the first person singular, asks, "Ah, what shall I write?" Readers of David Jones immediately recognize the first line of "A,a,a, Domine Deus," one of his very few short poems and the initial piece in *The Sleeping Lord*. The 1966 revision extracts fourteen lines of verse and seven lines of prose from the conclusion of *The Book of Balaam's Ass*. If it were not a prayer in its new form, it would be a confession of total despair. In its original context, all of the verse lines are part of the prose where "I have journeyed among the dead forms causation projects from pillar to pylon," where "I have felt for his wounds in nozzles and containers . . . have tested the inane patterns . . . for it is easy to miss Him at the turn of a civilization." This is all, with slight modifications, in "A,a,a, Domine Deus." But in the original version we are at this moment confronted with a passage that seems more William Burroughs than David Jones. "I have opened my heart to sterility when she said, 'Ain't I nice with me flexible flanks . . . You can, given the equation, duplicate me any number of times.'" The speaker here is some kind of android prostitute, a kind of being that only inhabits the Zone. Love, along with play, prayer, and praise, has no place here. A voice says: "We also have them in Dominican buck . . . but I advise our other model, the Odalisque. It's identical with our occidental pattern but frosted in Caucasian cellophane." What follows sounds like a set of instructions of how one might play with a condom – mentioned earlier in the text – as with a kind of rubber ribbon. "You can hold it in your hand / You can tie it in a knot / You can swing it to and fro . . . Can't we send it sir, to any address?"

In our youth we all thought of a zone as some *where* (if not quite some *place*) good to be, perhaps weird and a little frightening on first encounter, but not a kind of "Mortmere" (as Christopher Isherwood and Edward Upward called their shared zone at Cambridge) where everything was turned upside down and inside out and every kind of abnormality and disorder made to seem the only order of the day – as it also seemed to be when we encountered Burroughs as prefigured by David Jones in the aftermath of World War I. As Isherwood wrote, recounting Upward's renunciation of Mortmere, "The kind of literature which makes a cult of violence, sadism, bestiality and sexual acrobatics is peculiarly offensive and subversive in an age such as ours which has witnessed the practically applied bestiality of Belsen and Dachau." One figure who would have been right at home, or even a facilitator, in the Zone on the heath near Winchester, would have been Burroughs' "A.J.," "the notorious merchant of sex." He arrives as an agent at the Duc de Ventre's ball "as a walking penis covered by a huge condom." He consorts with "the Ergot Brothers, who decimated the Republic of Hassan with poisoned wheat, and Autopsy Ahmed and Hepatitis Hal, the fruit and vegetable brokers." As nearly everybody now knows, almost everything in *Naked Lunch* has to do with addiction: to drugs, beauty, sex, power, virtue, or art. Interzone and its four political parties seemed to us in 1959 like a madman's version of Eisenhower's America where the market – whether for produce or securities or prostitutes – swarms with "replicas," which, like David Jones' androids, are forever delivered into temptation's way by the nature of things.[2] Lunchtime news of

_____

[2] I note in passing that such fully life-size android sex workers are suddenly on the imminent commercial horizon and doubtless already available to early investors in certain American zones.

Interzone activities originating in "Bill's Diner" was a revelation and a prophecy that one could pick up, like the author himself, and like a message to Orpheus from the underworld, on "a 1920s crystal set."

I have digressed a good deal, but the point has been that zoning issues taken up by authorities very far away in time and space from my Glen Echo ravine harkened for their inspiration sometimes to a malign muse. However, Andrei Tarkovsky's *Stalker*, perhaps the greatest artifact ever actually "set" in a zone, and identified as such, could almost have been filmed in Glen Echo itself. By the time I knew anything about Tarkovsky, Goss and Barkan had both departed the scene, leading lives more useful to the real world of practical endeavor and ethical conduct than mine would ever be. I have continued always to seek out zones.

I am not the only person to have the sense that Tarkovsky's *Stalker* – by which he means something like a guide – could have been filmed in the local landscape of his youth. Geoff Dyer in *Zona*, a book devoted entirely to *Stalker*, remembers along the way how much Tarkovsky's zone recalled an area near Chelthenham where he grew up. There was an abandoned railway station and a brambly area where he played with friends. There were broken slabs of concrete structures that once served some utility company. And many other props from Tarkovskyland. When Stalker leads his two initiates into the Zone – the actual filming having been done near Tallinn, Estonia, by the Jägala River – I always see a kind of triple exposure – teenaged Barkan, Goss, and Matthias plodding along Glen Echo Creek with its overhanging trees, high weeds, and collapsed buildings of some kind, along with what remained of a frame house that had actually fallen down the cliff side on which it was at some point securely perched and looking over, but also a much younger and costumed group of kids, my cousins Robert and Richard, with myself as guide. The ravine, even in those early years when we ranged in ages from eight to twelve, was understood to by my zone.

Tarkovsky did not like his films to be interpreted. When the stalker and his companions – a professor and a writer – arrive in what may be the excluded area of a meteor's strike, a war of some kind, or even something supernatural, the viewer is torn between just letting the ruined power plants, rusted rail lines, lush green vegetation, sodden marshes, echoing tunnels, and all the rest just be themselves, while noticing, all the same, the old quest theme leading to a "room" which even seems rather like the Grail Castle as evoked in *The Waste Land* and *In Parenthesis*. Outside the door, Stalker recites a poem by Tarkovsky's father, Arsenii, a significant Russian poet and younger contemporary of Mandelstam, Tsvetaeva, and Akhmatova, to all of whom he dedicated memorial poems.[3] Stalker's voice undergoes the kind of change we have grown used to when a Russian has been talking and then begins to read or recite a Russian poem. The refrain line, difficult for the translator, is roughly "Yet surely there's more." But is there? Kitty Hunter Blair, Arsenii Tarkovsky's translator, urges us to read poems of the filmmaker's father in the tradition of "a kind of music," as a "mathematical" rather than an allegorical symbol. Blair notes that not long before the poem is recited, Stalker "talks of music as the purest of the arts because it expresses only itself." Even the shot of a pilgrim putting on a crown of thorns may exist only as a kind of dare: Don't try to interpret this any more than the broken telephone poles, the abandoned tunnels, or the telephone in the room that still seems to be working.

Nonetheless, we are in a zone. Again, Dyer gets it just right. When do we arrive? "We are in the Zone when we believe we are there." And: "It is every bit as lovely as Stalker claims while at the same time quite ordinary." Speaking about the same kind of experience, Roy Foster notes that Jorge Luis Borges believed that "the surface of reality occasionally opens a tiny crack into 'the

---

[3] Absolutely essential to the relationship between the filmmaker and his father is Kitty Hunter Blair's *Poetry and Film: Artistic Kinship between Arsenii and Andrei Tarkovsky* (London: Tate Publishing, 2014). Blair translates all of Arsenii's poems recited in Andrei's films, along with many others. At his best, as far as one can judge the translations, Arsenii was a fine poet. *Stalker* fans also should probably read *The Roadside Picnic* by Arkadi and Boris Strugatsky, the chief literary source of the film. Meanwhile, a video game exists in which *Stalker* and Chernobyl merge in a highly inventive zone that the player can enter and then participate. See GSC Game World, *S.T.A.L.K.E.R.: Shadow of Chernobyl* (THQ, 2007).

possibility of an entirely other order of things.'" But as Robert Hass sees in *Twentieth Century Pleasures,* the "entirely other order" must be, finally, an aspect of the entirely real: "Art hardly ever [seems] to come to us first as something connected to our own world; it always seems to announce the existence of another, different one, which is what it shares with Gnostic insight. That is why the thing that artists have to learn is that this world *is* the other world."

Like many others, I only read Svetlana Alexievich after she unexpectedly won the Nobel Prize. Her *Voices from Chernobyl: The Oral History of a Nuclear Disaster* is, like *Stalker,* about a zone of exclusion. We are never sure why Stalker's zone is excluded by the authorities to the extent that armed police and military fire at the three pilgrims who sneak into the forbidden area. We do know that the Zone has in some way crippled Stalker's daughter and led to the suicide of his mentor, known as Porcupine, whose trail Professor, Writer, and Stalker are so careful to follow as if, should they stray, they would all be blown up by buried land mines.

One of the interviews in *Voices from Chernobyl* is with a cameraman sent to document the disaster. Already, villages have been evacuated leaving empty houses looking as if their owners had just stepped out for a moment — like, in fact, the houses in the episode of *The Twilight Zone* called "Where Is Everybody?" The cameraman says, "I want to explain this whole other dimension . . . Dust. I already knew this wasn't just dust, but radioactive dust. I started filming apple trees in bloom. The bumblebees are buzzing and everything is bridal white . . . And I got this sense that everything was false . . . that I was on a film set."

Dyer notes that it is Professor, not Stalker himself, who proclaims, "the birth of a myth or religion: a place where something may or may not have happened; a place with a power that was intensified — possibly even created — by being forbidden." I know that our parents were frightened by our overwhelming desire to "go down the ravine." The only thing that was ever said was "Don't go all the way to the river." We always did. For fifty years, in one way or another, I've tried to write about that experience. Nothing since that time has approximated it as — as what? A rationally inexplicable aesthetic or metaphysical "walking into clarity," as the English composer and poet Ivor Gurney wrote from an asylum after the First World War of his own remembered Gloucestershire.

When Stalker, Professor, and Writer know they are in the Zone, black and white changes to color. That's as good a figure for transcendence as any. And yet when they get to the room, there's not much there but an antique telephone that somehow can still dial in the outside world. The phone, the radio, the camera, and other mechanical means of connection – these exist in the other zones I've written about here, and in some cases dominate the human visitors. As for me and my two young cousins and my two older friends, it's hard to say. In fact it's impossible to say. It was all good-and-bad, bad-and good, good, bad, beyond all that. It was sometimes a joke, sometimes an earnest waking dream, sometimes a dance or a dare. A few artists and writers caught a corner of it. Nothing was ever again as remarkable as where we had been. Like the stalker, I've looked for ways to go back. If I was ever there to begin with.

III

Prynne and a Petoskey Stone
and
First and Last Opinions,
with Parentheticals

Prynne and a Petoskey Stone

1

Prynne and a Petoskey Stone
is, I know, a fairly ridiculous title; and yet
it came about quite naturally. It also has what
Edward Dorn once said about a line of his own
on Charles Olson, "a good syllabification,"
not to mention nice alliteration: Let it preen
as you say it: *Prynne and a Petoskey Stone.*
The White Stones, a book by Prynne, arrived
in the mail from NYR Editions reprints,
a version of the Grosseteste original, 1969.
I've known the book since then, but wanted
to see what it looked like gizzied up and
canonized: introduction, index of first lines,
and all that sort of thing. I was so keen to see it,
in fact, that I had it sent to Walloon Lake, MI,
where I'm vacationing. From the same box
on the same day I also fished *A Complete*
Guide to Petoskey Stones. Now you understand.
No one could resist *some* kind of association,
absolutely on the spot. Imagine walking back
to Prynne's favored Pleistocene – a phase
that is "our current sense" – all the way from
the Devonian and Carboniferous, four hundred
million years ago, more of less, to us.

2

Pebbles on my mantle are
from Aldeburgh beach and neither white
nor from a coral petrified in time then broken
by the weight of glaciers, bottom washed
in shallow water from the Gulf of Mexico
to Michigan. The mantle stones are choir:
mixed among them are some jagged pieces
of Berlin's broken wall, flaking off
the red and blue of a protester's paint.
The wall fell. The corals on Petoskey shores
arrived as *hexagonaria percarinata,* leaping
from the Paleozoic to hex new hominids and
brother creatures on the Ellsworth shale.
My Aldeburgh stones recall the choral singing
at the Orford church, the stones from Berlin
a chapter of our inhumanity. And JHP's NYR
white stones? I'd pass him a Petoskey in exchange
for one. Exchange is his subject, and profound
as weight or measure in the alchemy of night.

3

In fact, my awkwardness includes a dizzy head
of syllables attempting dance, a breathless
hunting for the line. Once at his college, I wore
a borrowed gown and spilled my glass of wine
to high table merriment, but still I thought it
was a fond libation. The old poet is over eighty
and undaunted. Even I am halfway through
my own eighth decade now. Not so long, declares
the gay geologist of one's imagination. Gay
in Yeats's sense, not in the sense of our
contemporary speech. In America, I said,
we have but *low* tables, though often high style
in spite of that. May the college please forgive
my spillage and its mopping up. Look, I said,
I'll put this pocket full of white stones among
Petoskeys and the Aldeburghs, I'll even put
them in my mouth for eloquence. At the state
fair in Ohio, there was a contest for the
spitters forth of watermelon seeds – a serious
art where I grew up – and one year the eight yards
covered by my seed won me second place.
Imagine what I could have done with these
smooth stones from Aldeburgh and Petoskey,
or white ones from a book. I'd honor certain poets
and their places that's for sure,
but also claim my distance *fffffust fffffust fffffust*.

4

Ovoid with a kind of swollen belly, the unpolished
stone caught my eye one morning in the
shallow lappings of the lake. I picked it up and
brushed its egg-shaped surface with a cloth, washed
it with Chablis I carried in my bag. If a stone can
be said to have a top, its highest hexagons began
to shine in all their mathematical precision
and their pre-configuration of a Fuller geodesic
dome as its corals, formed when only fish could see,
evolving from extraordinary violence — birds
and dinosaurs, the first primates, mammoths,
all now above the deep shale over which an ice
of quaternary glaciers lay — raised questions to be
only left unsolved —

5

                    What is the answer, then?
Or, as Miss Stein said, what's the question?
"Left unsolved" are questioners who are outlasted
by all stones, even by the concrete pieces of a wall
destroyed by the young when they, born among the
warring clans, started getting old. My daughter picked
up pieces, brought them home. Asked what degree
of failure a poet might endure, one could refer to
a man out of Idaho, whose 'Problem of the Poem
for My Daughter, Left Unsolved' could signify
a white stone, like a pearl and a diamond sometimes
signify a daughter left behind or running on ahead.
Or like Petoskey coral and an Aldeburgh pebble
might, placed together on a mantle piece,
taken from their seas and washed by human
hands, could also signify in ways that are transient
but more than transitive. Corals choired in
the shallow sea that covered our peninsula before
it moved from the equator to below the UP bridge.

A high stable stile – is there such a thing?
Circe's chosen cannot reach it, so they spit
their stones at undergraduates ranged in
hungry rows below the stage. I show
my one Petoskey and my several Aldeburghs
but am not admitted. In desperation's dream, I show
my daughter's two pieces of The Wall, and
then awaken in the People's Pub. Privileged there,
I buy a pint and point to a portrait on the wall
of a poet in his prime: That was me ('twas I)
when young I say to fellow geezer at the bar.
Would you believe it? I carried with me then a
pocketful of white stones and put them
in my mouth when I would speak. They were
like manna and they fed the midwestern mind:
I spoke from *The Torrents of Spring* and told
of Yogi Johnson, Scripps O'Neil, and the waitress
at the beanery, 1926, Charles Scribner's Sons, and
of a man who said his father was at Eton with
a Gladstone bag in Wellingtons, all sourced in
self-important Earnest Sherwood. They showed
me their Petoskey stones, one found at the cutbank,
one in a gravel pit, one at Cathead Point, and one at
the Sleeping Bear Dunes. They passed around the
220 and 600 grit, aluminum oxide and felt cloths
for buffing, messing up the job in a rush to finish with
a thin application of transparent fingernail polish.
(My text, I was certain, had lacked polish,
was like my manners with the college wine.)

Do we emerge from melon seeds as Chinese
singing in *Shijing* maintain, in Arthur Waley's version,
that we do? I spat my contribution in Columbus once
with that question left unsolved from
pre-dynastic Zhou, returning to a memory.
I'm also puzzled by the pieces of the wall;
just what do they mean? 'A Stone Called Nothing'
is the fifth to last title in the final pages of the
old Grosseteste book, signed in 1969, three fifty-six
of four seventy-seven copies printed, Number 1,
Stonefield Avenue, Lincoln UK, set in ten point
Plantin type: *You say I / think or not /
get on / get off / quiet / match the stone.* I note,
like some Confucian sage, that melon seeds
bring melons, peach seeds peaches, cherry seeds
the cherry trees that blossom here; I'd pour
a quick libation, pocket pebbles from the Aldeburgh
beach if I were there. Here, I'll shine the corals
petrified by time and left behind by melting glaciers
still receding, which eventually will make this
shore and all the inland reaches of our low lying land
once again a warm and shallow sea.

First and Last Opinions, with Parentheticals

E. S. M., 1915

On October 21, 1915, the defendant
In error, filed her petition. She speaks of
Her husband who represented to her
That he was the owner. Of the house.

The same was unencumbered except
By the mortage. If the plaintiff would
Assume the payment of said and
Would pay to him a sum. Of $2,000

In monthly installments. As an inducement
To plaintiff to accept his offer aforesaid
He represented to her. No foundation of
Any house could be less. Or more than

Two and a half feet from. And that now
Double or two-family house, terrace,
Or apartment could be. (As for himself,
He's represented by his opinions; good

Ones and bad ones, depending on how
you'd excuse or justify the judgments
of the judge as conditioned by the times.
Opinions about Negroes. About Jews.

Even those about the Wops & Wogs and other
Late arrivals on these shores. He had a high
Opinion of his family, of himself. He asserted
That the name was German. There were

No indigenous Welsh Matthiases, even
If they only had one t. It's true, the press

Always called him a "brilliant jurist"
And "Dean of Ohio judges." His opinion

Of his eldest son diminished, but his
Opinion of his eldest daughter increased.
His second son also became a judge.
His second son sat in his father's chair.)

J. M. M., 1955

The plaintiff pleads, that while
Witnessing a baseball game he was
Injured when a player named
Philip Hudson negligently, carelessly,

And recklessly, and with great force
And violence, struck plaintiff in the left
Eye with a baseball, when said baseball
Player was wearing a uniform which

Bore the name *Delta Savings and Loan
Association.* Plaintiff alleges further
That the uniform and equipment being
Used by this player at the time of injury

Were owned by defendant and furnished,
Maintained and provided to and for
Said members of said baseball team for use
In attracting crowds and assemblages

Of people by playing baseball games,
Whereby said baseball players advertised
And promoted defendant's said business.
Plaintiff then prays that defendant be

Held liable to him in damages for this injury.
(Even I remember this one: a joke at dinner
when I was fourteen. Not so funny the times
he upheld death in capital offenses. Not by

baseball but by electric chair. They might
have tried it by baseball, I suppose. Rather
like stoning, it would take more than one
pitch. We kids played games sometimes

about "giving someone the chair." But
we saved the baseballs for baseball itself.)
He had opinions like his father, exactly
Like his father. He was not in the Spanish War,

But his opinion was that it was a "good thing,"
Not the occasion when the Old Republic was lost
Forever and forever and forever. His father was
Commander-in-Chief. Of all those vets who went

To Cuba and the Philippines, though he himself
Got no farther than a boot camp before the end
Of the war. Nonetheless, his influence got the
Benefits improved for all those Jingoes. J. M. M. was

Of the opinion that his father was a "great man."
This was also the opinion of all his siblings.
J. M. M. was on the court because E. S. M. threw
Himself out of a third story window. *Whoosh* . . .

E. S. M., 1953

. . . and then *thud.* Or *crash.* And my grandmother
Who had been swinging herself gently on the porch
Calling out *Oh Ed my God Ed what have you done?*
(No one else called him Ed. "Ed" was the first

Son, unable to get out of his chair because of
World War I, in which he never fought. But he was
Billeted in the barracks where the post-war
Spanish flu broke out, and it might have been

For the best had he died of it. Of the flu.
Thousands of others did. But he lived
On with *encephalitis lethargica,* "Sleeping Sickness"
As they called it, and his wife — if he was

Married — ran off in the night and disappeared.
Ed, Oh Ed . . .) And the distinguished jurist's
Last opinion, five justices concurring (and one
"Not participating." Why not?) declares concisely

That the rule is well established in this state
That a court of record speaks only through
Its journal and not by oral pronouncement
Or a mere minute or memorandum. It follows

That the court of appeals was in error.
Judgment reversed. He also mentions a
Vacation of judgment, or any vacation
At all. (He never took them, vacations,

He was always at his work with well
Established rules, writing for the record
Speaking only through a journal and not
By oral pronouncement, except in his family

Where, as I remember it, oral pronouncements
Were common enough, mainly about his
Opinions, never vacated, never a vacation, just
His work. The papers said he "fell.")

J. M. M., 1970

This one not about baseballs and baseball
Games, but the Jewell Company; not as funny as
His first opinion, but since it was his last,
We'll quote: Appellant operates what he calls

A Home Shipping Service. The truck is used
By his salesmen. Each salesman calls on his
Customers every other week unless he sleeps
Too long, or is drunk on the job. There are

Three types of sale: *impulse* sale, *tentative*
Order sale, and *catalogue* sale. I feel somehow
That I am sailing away. The cause is before
This court. The cause is always lost. At sea, on sail,

Impulsive or tentative. Our review is limited to
A determination. As if I were determined
To survive in catalogue, we reach the real question
Raised in this appeal: Am I too tired to go on?

The Commissioner's rule is relative to
The use of sale vehicles, not ships — sinking
Or still afloat (and in the end his license did
Run out): We argue with the board that upon

The above set of facts it is clear. That the
Applicant has not established that the truck
In question was a ship, or was entitled to
Exemption under the statute for sailing so

Far beyond the Commissioner's rule without
A pilot on board. So far from port. So fair a ship
She was and I was very tired. At just this point.
I remember law clerks, all of them good mates,

All of them bright men; some were barely more
Than boys. (For some time they had written his
Opinions, or most of them.) Must have been.
To the end he said: You are the last of my mid-

Shipmen to depart under rule of mortality.
(The rule of morality sometimes has no place
In law): His opinions sometimes not his own.
Was he only the shadow of his father's factor-

ing of this and that? Of his son's penciled mis-de-
méan-ors? He enjoyed his work on the Mú-ni-ci-pal Court
before his own father crashed to earth. Did that fall
Allow another's flight? He flew to occupy an un-ex-pir-

éd term. And his last o-pín-ion was
dé-livered from his bed (thought up
in his head
heart all full of lead) intended to be read

instead of *this*, and should be, certainly,
and well ahead of (what's-its-name the
rhyming word – deferred? Deterred?
(No last line, no opinion here, alas, at all . . .

and no closed parenthesis conferred

IV

Acoustic Shadows

. . . and it's not analogical at all —
for in *mirage* you see the line of troops that isn't there
and vanishes at your approach, whereas

Great-grand-sire Albert C. could hear the voice
of Ambrose Bierce from far away, deep in an Indiana outfit late
to join in the advance, but, like Grant and Sherman,

not the cannonades & fusillades that slaughtered thousands,
would have signaled strategies obscured in shadows
of the mind obscured by inability to hear

cannonades and fusillades that shattered adjuvant brigades.
No one heard the screaming wounded, Rebel yells, although
they saw well enough, in terms of awe and terror, all — as if some

silent movie, not yet technically achieved, played before the eyes
of Edward Shiloh, named by Albert C. for the balls-up horror of the
battle before Chickamauga and retreat to Chattanooga
                  after that.   *Sidebar 1*

Albert C. enlisted at sixteen, McComb, Ohio: Company K,
65th Ohio Volunteers. Ambrose Bierce, born in Meigs County,
                                     same state,
and just a little older . . . It is possible they met.

It is possible they met through an acoustic shadow, which allows
a man at great distance, now and then, to hear quite well what
                  a man
up close to the event itself cannot —

For example, me; for example, now.
And maybe Albert C. just there, just then; Biercings audible enough,
but not the roar and crash of civil war.

*

Ambrose Bierce, we need you at this hour!
But not in the version of *The Old Gringo*, Carlos Fuentes,
and the movie — no acoustic shadows — staring

G. Peck and J. Fonda — box office failure I'm told — for which
some text from *The Devil's Dictionary*
on a billboard all illuminated by

archaic gaslight might well serve anticipation.
Almost arbitrarily I put my finger down on *Valor*:

"Why have you halted," roared the commander
of a division at Chickamauga, who ordered a charge: "Move
forward sir at once." "General, said the commander of the
delinquent brigade, "I am persuaded that display of valor
will bring them into collision with the enemy."

We need you, Ambrose Bierce, man who disappeared.

Sidebar 1

Short news story, graphic
with the highlights of
a major one, something
incidental, conference
with the judge, lawyers,
sometimes the parties in
the case, which the jury
doesn't hear. Listen up.
What I saw at Shiloh, Shiloh,
wasn't what I'd name my
own offspring for, I can
sure tell you that. Came upon
the dregs of failed advance,
several thousand wounded
and defeated, beaten, cowed.
Deaf to duty, dead to shame.
All unconscious of their clay.
You may have built a family
on this chaos; me, I built a
style: None escaped, least
of all the earth. Bits of iron
stuck out of every tree,
knapsacks, swollen biscuits,
blankets beaten into soil
by the rain, rifles bent and
splintered stocks, waist-belts,
hats, heads, arms and legs,
a foot left running by itself,
an ear pinned to a wagon by
a broken bayonet, eyes of
one clutched in his open
hand as if on offer to us as
we passed him by and heard
the bugle-call, "assembly."

"All rise," says the bailiff
when the justices march in.
What justice for the dead?
No one rose, your honor, once
they fell upon the field, though
many prayed to god, the devil,
or (like me) the dictionary.

2

A file of troops is not like a line of verse
or a mirage in its advance/retreat and shape-changing
quatrain:

Shiloh
Stones River
Chickamauga
Resaca

A troop is not a trope though Grant and Sherman
sought to make a metaphor of early blunders
rather than to face a fact in plenary: a little boy with
wooden sword playing among casualties
and lost to what they both could hear and see but
then forgot —
                    A. C. Matthias & Lt. Ambrose Bierce,

child private and the brash volunteer recently
promoted to the tent of General Hazen as the new
topographical engineer, riding out alone to take the
measure of terrain, the good fields and bad

the good and bad possibilities of an advance, retreat

a retreat observed by the child with a wooden sword
an advance likely to become retreat

a treat for Christmas or his birthday, a wooden sword

although the engineer carried his sophisticated tools
he wrote, *Common paces 18*:

$$50' = 2\ 7/9'\ 2\ 7/9' = 2'\ 9\ 1/3$$

& preferred to pace rather than to use the chain
but liked his compass, leveling stick, circumference,
with the brass plates and tube to mount it.

Mountains were the worst for both of them, the enemy
dug in, entrenched. "Taking the high ground" was not
a figure of speech like shadow in acoustic shadow.

It was not a situation where one wanted to encounter,
for example, grape shot from artillery. Some commander might
insist one take the hill —

some commander like the one they called "Oh, No!"
or "General Prayerbook," the "Christian Officer" who managed
to outflank himself, his actions covered up at first but

called in good time "The Crime at Pickett's Mill."

Before that my forebear wrote: *We are very poorly clothed*
I have one blouse in rags, one pair of pants all full
of holes, and one pair of stockings which are always wet.

I feel sometimes that we ought to give the Rebs the South.
And we may have to do that anyway with generals
like our own who do not manage things. I advise, I do,

all men to stay at home, hiding if they must. We
forage here for all our food. Some have died of thirst.
The news is that Jeff Davis is in Murfreesboro —

while jumping backwards over time and space, the voice
jumping an acoustic shadow, his who had enlisted as
he left Ohio, trudged south from Elkhart —

                              These were men.
They crept upon their hands and knees. They used
their hands alone, dragging their legs.

They used their knees only, their arms hanging idly
at their sides. They came by dozens
and by hundreds, made gestures with their hands,

spread their palms upward in a kind of prayer.
But there was no help for these men
except for the child who walked among them

with a wooden sword and seemed unable to speak,
unable to hear. He made unholy sounds —
Gabbling like a turkey, chattering like an ape —

All the wounded took this as the voice of doom, Goddamn
death itself, dandified in costume, toy soldier come
to life, bearing upsidedowndrawn cross.

3

Goddamn the goddamn damn.
Edward Shiloh used to shout, stuck on an "opinion."
Was he his father's son?

Dear Son, wrote Albert C., dedicating
William Hinman's *Story of the Sherman Brigade.*
Carefully preserve this book that future

Generations of descendants
read and profit by it. I pray your generation
may know peace. But this is a story

of our suffering and tribulation. As Edward Shiloh
cursed and tore his hair, I'd open Hinman's book
and align my lead soldiers in configurations based on

battle maps: Shiloh, Stones River, Chickamauga
and Resaca. I collected hundreds of these poisonous toys,
and sometimes even licked them with my tongue,

loving them so much I'd want to taste them. I'd make
the hills and mountains, placing objects
underneath a carpet, then set up artillery and units of

reserves at the rear of both defenders and
the ones who would advance into the gatlings & grapeshot.
Then the cavalry at unexpected angles for

anticipated hit and run. With care I would align
Albert C.'s poor infantry, lines and lines of them, and then
some snipers in the trees. Finally, gray defenders

took their places in the hills. E. S. M.'s stone house was
on Iuka, named for yet another battle.

Shiloh on Iuka.
I think my grandfather had a kind of writer's block.

He could no more advance against his obstacle than my
lead version of his father could. I would never proceed to
the battle. I'd set them up according to my strategy,

which sometimes took me hours with the maps.
Goddamn the goddamn damn.
The house was so big, and I was so far away, that

sometimes I'd see him in a window where the walls
turned back on themselves, outflanking sense,
but not hear the blasphemies. I was in the library,

surrounded by three thousand books. *Do not lend* was

stamped on the *Ex Libris* plate of *The Story of the Sherman
Brigade.* In Van Wert, before the family moved
to the capital, his books outnumbered those in public

collections. I loved the smell of them. I still do.
Edward S. outlasted all of his contemporaries
on the court, setting records for tenure. He was remote.

His opinions are still read today. He killed himself
by jumping out the window where I'd watched
him pace and curse. At about the same age Ambrose Bierce

disappeared in Mexico. Or so they say.

Sidebar 2

Dear Justice E. Shiloh —
fuck you and your Jingo
vets. Ambrose Bierce here.
Here, there and up your —
well, whatever. I know
full well you never got
beyond some kind of
scout camp in Ohio,
but I knew your old man.
There was a brave hombre!
You, I've no idea. You were
Commander-in-Chief of what?
United Spanish-American
War vets? You, who never
fired a shot, were never
fired upon. Here's a bit I
wrote just for you. You
and John Marshall, your
son; John Edward, your
grandson, and even Ian
Bendoly, your great-grandson.
I was no leftie, Commander-
In-Chief, far from it, but the
Loss of the Old Republic that
T. R. and you and Hearst
achieved — talk about "fake news."
Said Citizen Hearst, my boss
at the time: "You write the stories,
I'll provide the war."
You fell for all of it. Granted,
you were young. But when you
were very old you still believed
the shit you thought when
you'd recite "A Toast to the Flag,"

in much the spirit Maoists waved
the "little red book" when your
grandson was in college.
Before the Journal *made me*
change my tune, I said "the
warmongering press has already
broken out like a red rash
in the papers, whose managing
Commodores are shivering
their timbers and blasting
their top lights with a
truly pelagic volubility."
Here's the opposite of
an acoustic shadow: noise
precedes events, sound moves
faster than light, blather,
blather, bosh, and blah blah blah.
Watch this column for
another sidebar soon.

4

My mother used to claim, "It jumps a generation," and
that is, unlike *mirage*, analogous – I mean it's like the notion
of acoustic shadow in its way.

I will explain. Or maybe I already have
but failed myself to hear, as a result of concentrating
on the explanation in the way "Oh, No!"

actually outflanked himself in spite of Bierce's
work as master of topography, frogs of leaping neurons
all befogged by conscious thought and not the fog

of war, attempts of will to jump the synchronizing
synapses, crossing over Oostanaula River in the night,
or jumping now a generation. *It* was the habit of

a magpie Song of Self derived from cuts and clippings.
We were our own press agents, Edward S. and I,
with scissor blades made for just the purpose of assisting

young poets and distinguished jurists in pursuit of
newspaper reference, blades almost the length of swords
that now reside among my fireplace tools on the

imitation Delft tiles that I unsheathe now and then
just to poke and prod a winter fire.
We both, Edward S. and I, would cut and slash,

pile the clippings in a box or paste them in a book.
My father didn't do this; his was the generation skipped.
Oostanaula River was below Resaca.

On a visit in my youth, I skipped stones across it.
Albert C. and Ambrose Bierce did not have
time for such child's play –

nor to download and print out a clipping from
abroad telling me again *it skips*
a generation as it skips across the sea out of

entombment in the etymologies: "deadline," for
example: a pile of mortal men beyond which
no advance is possible. Cf. "Lime pit," dug by survivors

after battle into which the rotting dead were heaved.

5

Albert C. downloaded a small ball and masticated wad
to hold it in the barrel while he peered
around a tree looking for an enemy to shoot.

But he was shot himself, his forearm left all dangling
from the elbow. Hillman writes that
Corporal Matthias, who was scarcely more than a boy

*Was wounded fighting only fifty yards from the
Confederate lines,* but Albert C. himself
has written in the margin: *Our position was a mere*

Twenty paces from their stone fort.
So his last battle was Resaca. The wounded arm
lasted, hanging paralyzed, for many years,

as he practiced medicine, sometimes riding
with a sidearm out to vaccinate
Ohio skeptics against smallpox and against their will.

In time, they cut the arm off at the elbow. He put
it in a bottle of preservative and wrote
a will, Goddamnit, saying that the arm must be

buried with the rest of him. Ambrose Bierce,
also wounded and experiencing hallucinations, migraines,
double vision, and the PTS they didn't understand

when they told him, "Goddamn it, pull your socks up,
soldier!" didn't march with Sherman to the sea.
For a while, he couldn't see to march.

Nor could Albert C. "get a grip on himself," as he
Was told — unable to move his hand or feel his arm.
"I'll wait till I see what I hear," Edward S. would say,

preparing for an oral argument, putting down the brief.
He'd come downstairs, exhausted, browse
Among his books, thumbing favorites absent-mindedly,

while I, waiting to hear what he saw, continued crawling
on the floor and moving toy soldiers in accordance
with the paragraphs about campaigns that I

only understood as fiction, sometimes confounded by
some facts my grandfather mumbled when he
took in all my strategies – "Father, Johnny, wasn't

where you've got him there. He was only twenty
paces from the stone fort of the enemy . . .
You've put him too far back. Goddamn lucky

(blasphemies of a judicial origin applied)
"he saved his life to start our clan."
Later, "Bitter Bierce" as he was called when

he began to write, was quoted in the *Hangtown Gibbet*
or the *Weekly Howl* saying, for example, in obits:
the cause of death was galloping Christianity of the

malignant type . . . or: After church last Sunday afternoon
a Chinaman was stoned from the steps of the
First Congregational Church. Other Christians drove

a crowbar into yet another's abdomen out of
sheer amusement. One arm was riven from its socket
by some great convulsion of nature. As the deceased

was seen enjoying his opium pipe and his usual health
just previous to the discovery of his melancholy
end, it is assumed he came by his death by heart disease.

This was San Francisco, where Bierce arrived, marching
to the sea in a direction opposite of Sherman.
By the time I pulled his *Devil's Dictionary* from the shelf

of Edward Shiloh's library, I could laugh at "Regalia" —
the Justice had so much of it that I'd try on,
admiring myself in the mirror on his closet door:

Knights of Adam; Visionaries of Detectable Bosh; Ancient
Order of Modern Troglodytes; League of Holy Humbug;
The Blatherhood of Insufferable Sloth; Associated Sovereigns

Of Mendacity; Dukes-Guardian of the Mystic Cesspool;
Order of the Undecipherable Scroll — "the distinguishing
insignia, jewels and costumes of such" —

and many more along with Edward Shiloh's Mason's
robes, his Captain's uniform as failed soldier
in the Spanish War, and in the backmost darkmost

depths of secret walk-in closet's secrets — Reliquary:
arms and legs, ears and eyes, fingers, teeth,
the beards of many generals, a penis, a pancreas, a spleen.

6

Splenetic, sometimes,

Albert wore his sanguinary arm just like a gifted relic,
hanging at his side. There wasn't much
a doc could do, even with both hands, for the sick

in Gilboa or McComb, towns where he set up
his practice having learned most of what
he knew from a long convalescence from the wound

in Nashville, Jefferson, Cleveland, and the office
of a Dr. Dean where he apprenticed when
still a patient himself. But for diphtheria, typhus,

even measles, there was little to do but watch.
Dean told him, "They feel better when
I walk in their door, but then they understand

we can't do anything but be there." It was
Dean who told him, "Pack a gun when
you vaccinate in the countryside. That way

they're less likely to keep you from their kids.
The hell with stupid parents. If they want to
die from smallpox, let them die." Bierce would

have liked this last remark and maybe even have
quoted it in his *Town Crier* column, or under his   *Sidebar 3*
pen name, "Ursus," in the *Grizzly Papers* as he

started being read. Even Albert C. read him
in Ohio, knowing him as veteran of the
battles he himself had fought and knowing him as

former resident of Meigs County. In McComb
and Gilboa, Bierce was read by some
who knew him or his reputation: One paper

called him "wise, witty, lively and severe."
Another was shocked at the "Rabelaisian audacity
of his homicidal prose." Albert C.'s books

ended up among the hundreds that I browsed
on Edward Shiloh's shelves. Right next
to Hinman's *The Sherman Brigade*, Bierce on

Shiloh, Chickamauga, Coulter's Notch, Resaca,
and the hanging at Owl Creek Bridge.
His journalism flayed the privileged and the

stupid and the blind, especially if they happened
to be Christian. Albert C. was Christian
but not dumb. He wanted to be paid. He had

a card for patients headed "Your Physician,"
reading thus: *He is a friend when a friend
is most in need. He does not like to disturb the ill*

*by collecting through the law. Make him feel
that he's appreciated. Promptly pay
his fee. He is a skilled and tired and busy man.*

A copy of this card marks a place in Bierce's
book. He's drawn and doodled in the
margins of his card: A wading marsh bird with

a long beak holds a kind of dangling banner
saying: "Ambrose Bierce. I met him after Chickamauga."
It marks a place where the handwriting changes

in the margins of the book itself. There's a story called
"Killed at Resaca," and A. C. M. has written his
familiar and insistent "Twenty paces from the enemy."

E. S. M. has written under that: "Not killed, but gravely
wounded. In and out of hospitals for months.
He always said he'd lied about his age." Blood ran from

the doctor's practice and from Bierce's books: In one
story swine stand on the bodies of the dead
and wounded, eating off their faces, one by one.

Sidebar 3

*Some telegrams (later to
be known as "tweets"): For
example (dictionary):* Realism,
*The art of depicting nature as it
is seen by toads; the charm of suf-
fusing a landscape painted
by a mole; a story written by
a measuring worm.* Reality, *I
say, is the dream of a mad
philosopher or what would
remain in the cupel if one
should assay a phantom — or
the nucleus of a vacuum:* Rear
*in the military is that exposed
part of the army nearest to the
Congress while* To reason *is to weigh
probabilities in the scale of
desire. And then there is* Ink:
*a villainous compound of tan-
nogallate of iron, gum-arabic, and
water, chiefly used to facilitate
the infection of idiocy and
promote intellectual crime. It
may be used to make reputations
and unmake them, to blacken
them and to make them white, but
it is most generally and acceptably
employed as a mortar to bind
together stones in an edifice of fame,
and as a whitewash to conceal
afterwards the rascal quality of the
material. All of this for you,* A. C. M.,
E. S. M., J. M. M., J .E. M.: *Gilboa, Columbus,
Elkhart, South Bend, other towns of*

the great American Midlandmind
unhinged on hinged porch swing
& madly swung by some phantom
swinger pushing patent medicines
and shouting arm, to arms, to arms.

7

Bierce courted an unlikely girl. Who would have guessed
he'd be smitten by a debutante, and even swear
to friends he was in love? "Love" in his Dictionary: "A temporal

insanity that's cured by marriage." It's not even clear
that he enjoyed sex, though Mollie did — and
possibly at first she liked his tales. Eros, for him, manifested

in his monologues, although eventually he told his stories
to his drinking friends and the pages of his books.
As Railroad Baron Jingoes took up absolute command,

he brooded, gasped for breath when asthma hit him
in the chest like bullets from a firing squad. He felt the full
force of panic, something Albert C. treated efficaciously

in Edward S. and might have treated in his friend from
Chickamauga. But who would start another war so soon after
the catastrophe that nearly killed the Union? Cuba,

the Philippines, Dewey's battleship . . . Bierce told his
wife about 'A Horseman in the Sky,' 'Four Days in Dixie,'
'One of the Missing,' 'Coup de Grâce.' When he met

Teddy R., the Rough Rider told him that his story called
'The Son of the Gods' inspired him on San Juan Hill,
up which he crawled on hands and knees like all the others

gasping for their breath, no equestrian at all, a question
maybe for E. S. who ended up with all the books
but never learned their lesson. Nor did I when I abandoned   *Sidebar 4*

toy soldiers on the carpet and put on the uniforms. *Death
to the Old Republic*, I might have cheered: *Hurrah
for the Empire* being born and my grandfather's trek

as far as training camp, but not beyond. It was a short
kind of war. Unlike Albert C., he never fired a shot,
was never shot at. Still, I loved the uniforms.

As for the Reliquary, Bierce omitted one left arm.
The Dictionary, though, lists *the ears of Balaam's ass,*
The lung of the cock that called Peter to repent,

a feather from the Angel of Annunciation, and the head
of Saint Dennis, arrived in Canterbury to explain
that it was seeking a body of doctrine, but thrown into

the Stour. Another head was ordered straight from Rome.
As for the arm, my own belief is that it took on life
and spent no time at all as relic in the closet, but after

amputation gave, ahead of its time and fully avant-garde,
a Fascist salute. *Viva la Muerte* was in fact a slogan
of Falangists. Oh severed arm, you had your own ideas

in spite of the will and determination of Albert C.
I see you stand up on your hand and walk toward the
horizon. *Which side are you on?* the old labor movement

song enquired. I ask again, but cannot hear a reply
as I see you wave, salute. Eventually I hear
when the acoustic shadow lifts: *Didn't I say, old boy,*

Viva la Muerte, Viva la Muerte, Viva la Muerte.

Sidebar 4

. . . a bar where I ordered Sarsaparilla,
not the straight shot of whisky that the
gunslingers downed before a
shootout on some dusty crossroads
in a movie set, or, acoustic shadow,
in slow-mo, TV. Me, I grew up with radio,
and that seemed miracle enough.
Half-asleep, I'd half-hear the extra
innings of a baseball game, waking in
the morning half-remembering who won.
On radio there's no acoustic shadow,
and you either listen or you turn it off.
I'd turn off kids outside my room
who called me to go biking down the glen.
More and more, I stayed up in my room.
I understand, long after, that family
members were "concerned" about me,
that is, about my isolation from a normal
childhood. They wanted me out playing
with the others on the street. I did
that now and then, but something was
always missing. I tried to see what
it was, but only later heard it. It was
a summons to the past. Every other kid
was looking forward, only I was hearing
back. The voices grew familiar, but
broke up in storms with inexplicable
noises, sometimes static simply due to
awkward fingers on the dial. Who had won
the game? Who had won the war? Who
conquered history and parsed the past?
I did, now and then, have the sense I'd seen
some things before the words arrived to
tell me what they were: The breasts of

the girl next door, the boy with a
broken nose running home without
his bike shouting some abuse about
the bully down the glen. The sound,
the sense of it, came late. Many things
I saw confused me, and so I shut myself
in my room to listen, waiting for a
door into the basement, time. Down
there my father shoveled coal, my
mother washed my dirty clothes
by hand. But when they rose into
the present and I saw them with
the others, why did they strike poses,
war-memorial like, why were they
walking in broad day? I listened to
the radio and opened wide my eyes.
"Infidel," said Ambrose, reading
from his book: "you who fail to revere
the cenobites, vicars, rectors, robots,
fufis, pumpoms, acolytes, imams,
beneficiaries, clerks, confessors, beadles,
fakirs, fakers, motherfukers, parsons,
Persons of Importance, priors, padres,
canons and divines. You hear, my brother,
who will wait to verify, you sleepy eye?"

8

I've ordered the CD from Netflix, put it on, but turned off
the sound: and there he is, *Gringo Viejo*, complete with
acoustic shadow. It's clear there's another war, there always

is, and massive casualties, there always are. Mexicans are
falling off their horses, people getting shot. Some
hacienda's set on fire, and there's the hero, or I suppose

the anti-hero, Bitter Bierce himself, Mr. Peck straight
from his gig as Atticus Finch in *To Kill a Mockingbird*.
This time crows and vultures do the mocking, Oh, and

there's the Virile Revolutionary, straight from central
casting, and his Poncho Villa cadres, all very fierce
in their sombreros. Jane Fonda's the schoolmarm, come

to teach the kids of the Mirandas, teaching, or so it
seems, the poor who have inherited, if not the earth,
the ranch. Peck's a little old for her, but she allows

one kiss. There seem to be prostitutes following
the progress of the volunteers, and plying their trade
from an empty railroad car. Jane takes some

lessons from them in the art of sex, ends up of course
with the "General," self-appointed, leaving Gringo Viejo,
Bitter Bierce, as father figure, not a lover.

To figure all this out requires no sound at all, unlike
those battles where acoustic shadow led to
catastrophic military errors. And this is how the past

comes at us, overwhelming us in image without
sound: old photographs, portraits, battle maps, nightmares
and silent films. I'd sit with others watching

home movies in my grandfather's house, and the
oldest would say: *Oh, there's Granny Crouch, there's
Uncle Ed.* We kids would shrug at these unspeaking dead,

walking there as if alive. We watched them talking
to each other, but of course we couldn't hear.
What did they say? What does Fonda say to Peck

and the Virile Revolutionary who, I think, may
be the black sheep of the Miranda clan who had owned
the expropriated hacienda. Me, I'd rather

sleep with the pretty whore than the schoolmarm.
That's what Bitter Bierce does in the end, gifting Jane
To "the revolution." At least that's what it looks like.

There are photographs of Albert C., but no scenes
with him in the movies. We only know what he said
from his letters and his dedication of

The Sherman Brigade. And there are newspaper clippings
in a box. We know what Bierce had to say
from his published stories and his rants. We don't know how

he ended up, and it's only speculation that he went to
Mexico at all. Still, why not think so? Writing this, I see that
the Virile Revolutionary's shot Mr. Peck in the back.

Jane is horrified, holds the dying man in her arms. If
I turned on the sound, I'd know what they were saying.
She maybe calls him "father." Peck couldn't

get his pecker up, although the whore let him feel
her breasts. Jane's "real" father died in Cuba
in the Spanish War. I can tell that from a flashback

without sound. Or did he? Maybe he just left
her mother for sexy Cuban girls and disappeared in dust
left over from the Spanish War. I turn on the sound

and *Las chicas cantan*, girls and whores. Shadow
blows away in a wind that gathers on the dry
horizon. Jane will bury Bitter Bierce in what

was meant to be her "real" father's grave. Peck
died at sea in *Moby Dick*, but this time no such luck.
This time he's Bitter Bierce, not Ahab.

Though already dead, he's tied up with the virile chap
who is, like revolutionaries everywhere, eaten by the movement.
Villa has them shot together, son and father one

is meant to think. What's a girl like Jane to do? She knows
little about Cuba, less about the Spanish War. Villa has
the gringo and the bastard Miranda shot together: what fun,

the end of a story, end of an Hacienda's line.
Unlike the others from my own Hacienda, I've no
love of Edward Shiloh's memory, just his house

and library, both now destroyed or lost along
with all my toy soldiers and his uniforms.
The war he trumpeted, like William Randolph Hearst,

was the end of something beautiful: The Old Republic,
saved by his own father, Bierce, and others
from Ohio and Indiana, ripe for betrayal by the

New Imperialists. *Remember the Maine*, they sang.
But *Las chicas cantan*. It's a different song
and one I'd rather sing. The Filipino jungles look

to me like those in Vietnam. In both they used
the water board, often just for fun. What would the good
doctor, A. C. M., have said about it all?

I'd throw his severed arm at the whole jingo lot of them.
The movie ends with Jane and Bierce's body on
a bridge over the Rio Grande. It's sunset, of course.

We are the stuff that beams of light are
made on; the stuff of reams of paper printed with
the ambiguities of words. We don't

hear very well. At least not what we see.

EPILOGUE

Blake's Painting *The Soul Hovering over the Body Reluctantly Parting with Life*

how

       how

            how I've loved you here
                   (you here)

            and yet I leave you there
                   (you there)

now

       now

            now because I must

                   (as dust, as dust)

Notes

Prologue. After Carlos Drummond de Andrade's "Lembrança do Mundo Antigo"

LEMBRANÇA DO MUNDO ANTIGO
[SOUVENIR OF THE ANCIENT WORLD]

Clara passeava no jardim com as crianças.
O céu era verde sobre o gramado,
a água era dourada sob as pontes,
outros elementos eram azuis, róseos, alaranjados,
o guarda-civil sorria, passavam bicicletas,
a menina pisou a relva para pegar um pássaro,
o mundo inteiro, a Alemanha, a China, tudo era
tranqüilo em redor de Clara.

As crianças olhavam para o céu: não era proibido.
A boca, o nariz, os olhos estavam abertos. Não havia perigo.
Os perigos que Clara temia eram a gripe, o calor, os insetos.
Clara tinha medo de perder o bonde das 11 horas,
esperava cartas que custavam a chegar,
nem sempre podia usar vestido novo. Mas passeava
no jardim, pela manhã!!!
Havia jardins, havia manhãs naquele tempo!!!

From Carlos Drummond de Andrade, *Sentimento do Mundo* (Rio de Janeiro: Editora Record, 1993), 170.
In Mark Strand's translation: "Clara strolled in the garden with the children. / The sky was green over the grass, / the water was golden under the bridges, / other elements were blue and rose and orange, / a policeman smiled, bicycles passed, / a girl stepped onto the lawn to catch a bird, / the whole world—Germany, China— / all was quiet around Clara. / The children looked at the sky: it was not forbidden. / Mouth, nose, eyes, were open. There was no danger. What Clara feared were the flu, the heat, the insects. / Clara feared missing the eleven o'clock trolley: / She waited for letters slow to arrive. / She couldn't always wear a new dress. But she strolled in the garden in the morning! / They had gardens, they had mornings in those days!" See Mark Strand, *Looking for Poetry: Poems by*

Carlos Drummond de Andrade and Rafael Alberti and Songs from the Quechua (New York: Alfred A. Knopf, 2002), 22.

Elevenses

Although I've only heard the term in the UK — it refers to a little break in the late morning for tea, a snack, a little conversation — the context here is strictly American.

Meeting Czesław Miłosz, 1984

The record has it that, while attempting to translate some late Miłosz poems, Robert Hass received a call from Kraków. A headnote in Hass's *Time and Materials* explains. When Miłosz asked the difference between *Oh!* and *O!*, Hass told him that *Oh!* was a long breath of wonder, that the equivalent was, possibly, "Wow!" and that *O!* was a caught breath of wonder and surprise, more like "Huh!" Miłosz said the solution was *O!* "for sure."

Oh, Wow!
Huh? O! For sure.

I sent these distinctions to a friend and scholar who has written on the subject himself. He replied:

> I have things to say about apostrophe and presence in the new critical book from CUP next year. Did you know that Prynne challenges Culler's old orthodoxy about apostrophe in his British Academy Wharton lecture by asserting that in the practices of poets such as Wordsworth (and many more, I should say), the vocative "O" is not wholly disambiguated from the exclamatory "oh," which is how apostrophe in poetic practice is often reconciled with an implication of presence, as in the "O sea" of Tennyson's 'Break, Break, Break' for instance. It matters to me because a support for properly occasioned speech acts in poems.

To which I answered:

> I've just founded a new literary movement to confound all proponents of both "Oh!" and "O!" This is

"Negationism – Negationists begin all apostrophes with O,
i.e. Zero:
As in:
O trees and lakes, O mountains and rivers,
O deep gorges and narrow paths through O wild nature,

etc.

Acoustics Zones Shadows
The source of the epigraph and several of the paraphrased lines is
Wallace Stevens' 'Connoisseur of Chaos.'

What's Left on Iuka Drive
September 19, 1862 was the date of the Battle of Iuka in the American Civil War.

Unpublished Letter to the *New Yorker*
Since writing this I have discovered that there was a second Professor Wisdom, who taught at Cambridge rather than London University. I have hesitated to investigate this, since the little story could become very Borgesian very quickly. Let us hope that our Professor Wisdom was the right one.

Changing Your Seat
The initial five and a half lines are from Michael Anania's poem 'Continuous Showings.'

Ashbury
Mortmere was the fictitious village invented by Christopher Isherwood and Edward Upward while students at Cambridge that appears in their early collaboration on a series of fantasy or surrealist stories, only some of which survive.

There Was a Plan
"Waiting for something to happen" is the last line of Michael Anania's poem 'Second-Hand Elegy.'

Like William Carlos Williams
The lines quoted from David Jones appear in his poem 'The Tutelar of the Place.'

Octaves
This version of two stanzas from Osip Mandelstam's 'The Age' differs from those appearing in my translation of the full poem in the book *Revolutions: A Collaboration* (with Jean Dibble and Robert Archambeau).

Some Zones
Footnotes in the essay/memoir itself are for information, not reference. Longer passages cited are from the following: Rod Serling, *Stories from the Twilight Zone*, edited by Anne Serling, pp. 70, 72, 84, xi, x; Wikipedia, s.v. 'The Shadow' last modified September 29, 2017, 00:43, https://en.wikipedia.org/wiki/The_Shadow; Carrie Noland, *Poetry at Stake: The Aesthetics and Challenge of Technology*, p. 143; Geoff Dyer, *Zona: A Book about a Film about a Journey to a Room* (Vintage ed.), pp. 73–92; Robert Hass, *Twentieth Century Pleasures*, p. 222; Svetlana Alexievich, *Voices from Chernobyl: The Oral History of a Nuclear Disaster* (Picador ed.), pp. 107, 106.

Prynne and a Petoskey Stone
See both editions of J. H. Prynne's *The White Stones*: Grosseteste Press, 1969 and NYRB Poets, 2016, which includes, in addition to the poems in the Grosseteste book, the poem 'Day Light Songs,' the essay 'A Note on Metal,' and an introduction by Peter Gizzi. For Petoskey stones, see Bruce Mueller and William H. Wilde, *The Complete Guide to Petoskey Stones*.

First and Last Opinions, with Parentheticals
Legal language sourced, modified, and distorted from the first and last Ohio Supreme Court opinions of Justices Edward S. and John M. Matthias, taken from Ohio State Reports and bound in eight volumes now residing in the archive of the Supreme Court of Ohio Law Library.

Acoustic Shadows

Chief source of information relating to the experiences of Albert C. Matthias during the Civil War is *The Story of the Sherman Brigade*, by Wilbur F. Hinman, "Published by the Author, 1897." The Sherman in question was John Sherman, not his brother William. Albert C. inscribes a presentation copy to his son Edward S.: "Christmas 1897. The story of the Sherman Brigade from November 8th 1861 to May 14th 1864, when I was wounded, is the history of my service in the war of 1861–1865. I was never absent from my command a single hour, never sick, never excused from duty until wounded. I did my duty on every march, in every battle and skirmish in all its hardships and privations. Carefully preserve this book, that future generations of our descendants may read and profit by it. Affectionately, Your Father, Albert C. Matthias, M.D." The 'Sidebars' are spoken by the voice of Ambrose Bierce, and they collage bits and pieces of his *Civil War Stories* (Dover Editions) and *The Devil's Dictionary*. Details of Bierce's life derive from various sources, but chiefly from Roy Morris, Jr.'s *Ambrose Bierce: Alone in Bad Company*. For legends, inventions, and apocrypha regarding Bierce's supposed career during the Mexican Revolution after his disappearance from the United States, see Carlos Fuentes, *The Old Gringo*, and Luis Puenzo's film of the same name.

Epilogue. Blake's Painting *The Soul Hovering*
over the Body Reluctantly Parting This Life
William Blake (1757–1827), *Soul Hovering over the Body*, 16.0 x 22.7 cm. Illustrations for Robert Blair's 'The Grave' (composed 1805), object 9. William Blake Archive. http://www.blakearchive.org/copy/butwba10.1?descId=butwba10.1.wc.09.

The illustration here is the engraving (1813) by Luigi Schiavonetti from Blake's original.

CPSIA information can be obtained
at www.ICGtesting.com
Printed in the USA
LVHW051120200120
644155LV00004B/601

9 781848 616363